# SET APART FOR SERVICE

# SET APART FOR SERVICE

## ALTON H. McEACHERN

**BROADMAN PRESS**
Nashville, Tennessee

"Stopping By Woods on a Snowy Evening" by Robert Frost is from *Poetry of Robert Frost,* edited by Edward Connery Lathem, Copyright 1923, © 1969 by Holt, Rinehart and Winston, © 1951 by Robert Frost, reprinted by permission of Holt, Rhinehart and Winston, Publishers.

Scripture quotations marked NEB are from *The New English Bible.* Copyright © The Delegates of the Oxford University Press and the Syndics of the Cambridge University Press, 1961, 1970. Reprinted by permission.

Quotations marked Phillips are reprinted with permission of Macmillan Publishing Co., Inc. from J. B. Phillips: *The New Testament in Modern English.* © J. B. Phillips 1958, 1960.

Quotations marked RSV are from the Revised Standard Version of the Bible, copyrighted 1946, 1952, © 1971, 1973.

Dewey Decimal Classification: 253
Subject heading: ORDINATION

Library of Congress Catalog Card Number: 79-51140
Printed in the United States of America

TO

# S. C. RAY

My colleague and partner
in ministry

# Preface

This study was undertaken at the suggestion of Robert Hastings, editor of *The Illinois Baptist*. He noted the lack of printed material on Baptist ordination practices. I am grateful for his encouragement.

Mrs. Dorothy Holleman has served faithfully and efficiently as typist in the preparation of this manuscript.

I am also grateful to friends who have shared ordination sermons, orders of service, and other materials included in chapter 5.

The First Baptist Church of Greensboro, North Carolina, and its associate pastor, S. C. Ray, have been gracious in their help with this undertaking.

While this book takes note of some of the scholarship on the subject of ordination, its purpose is quite practical. I hope it contributes to a clearer understanding of the Baptist practices of ordination. It does offer some useful suggestions both to those being ordained and those conducting ordination councils and services. Ordination is a highly significant experience in the life of a candidate and in the worship of the church. I will be gratified if this work contributes in some measure to both.

ALTON H. MCEACHERN
Greensboro, N.C.

# Contents

# 1.
# The Biblical Basis
# of Ordination

Ordination is the initial rite by which the church sets apart an individual to the Christian ministry. It is almost a universal practice within the church. Yet, there are widely diverse opinions as to the significance of ordination, even among Protestant denominations. While practiced by Baptists, there appears to be no concensus among us as to its precise meaning.

## Ordination as Installation

Some view ordination lightly, as merely the symbolic installation of a man in a place of ministry. Thus, it becomes virtually a meaningless ritual of limited significance.

## Mystical View

Others being ordained experience it as a time of personal spiritual significance. It becomes a time for self-examination and confession of sin. It is an act of dedication to the Lord and to the place of service given by his grace. For these persons ordination to the ministry is roughly equivalent to the knight's vigil on the eve of his induction into knighthood. This could be considered a mystical view of the significance of ordination.

## Institutional View

Still others have an institutional understanding of ordination. It elevates a man to a new status with position, authority, and power. He is expected to be more pious and less human after this ritual—a member of "the third sex." From the church's point of view, ordination can elevate the candidate to a "super Christian" plane. The ordinand's ego may become inflated when he and the church have such a high view of the importance of ordination (or of the person ordained).

## Magical View

In the wider history of the church, ordination has been viewed almost magically. Authority (the keys of the kingdom) was conveyed to the man ordained. His actions as priest were considered valid despite the flaws in his personal character. Such a view of the significance of ordination is far afield from Scripture.

## Toward a Biblical View

As people of the Book, Baptists seek to base their beliefs and practices on Scripture. It becomes a bit disconcerting when one attempts to uncover the roots of ordination within the Bible—there is little crystal clear evidence for it. However, the early roots are to be found there.

Wayne E. Ward contends that the current practice of ordination to the Christian ministry has developed far beyond anything to be found in the Bible itself. Such is inevitable as the church grew and gave expanded definition to its beliefs and practices.

## The Laying On of Hands

The common point between "setting apart" in the Bible and the modern practice of ordination is the ritual of "laying on hands" and prayer. The meaning given the laying on of hands will vary within Scripture, as within modern ordination practices.

## Laying On of Hands in the Old Testament

This practice is found in the old covenant. It had three kinds of significance: The laying on of hands could be a sign of bestowing a blessing. It was also used to symbolize identification with the animal sacrificed, or to transfer guilt to the scapegoat. The rite could also have the significance of installation in a position of leadership. Let's examine some examples of these three meanings.

### Bestowal of a Blessing

This is the most common use of the laying on of hands in the Old Testament. In Genesis 27 we have the account of such an occasion.

The patriarch Isaac was growing old and his eyesight had failed. Feeling that the time of his own death must be near, he determined to give his blessing to his elder son, Esau. This blessing would convey the father's inheritance and leadership of the family. Thus, it had great significance. Once given, the blessing was irrevocable and legally binding.

Isaac's wife, Rebekah, favored Esau's twin brother, Jacob. She devised a scheme to get the family inheritance for her favorite. The Scripture writer gives a fascinating account of their deception of blind Isaac.

Jacob successfully carried out the deception of his blind father and received this blessing. Tension builds as the story goes along. Isaac said, "Come near, my son, and kiss me ... God give you dew from heaven/and the richness of the earth,/corn and new wine in plenty!/ Peoples shall serve you,/nations bow down to you. Be lord over your brothers;/may your mother's sons bow down to you./A curse upon those who curse you;/a blessing on those who bless you!" (Gen. 27:26-29, NEB).

Such an Oriental blessing was considered final (see Isa. 55:11). It could not be taken back even though it was given under false pretenses. The blessing was agricultural—promising that Jacob and his descendents would inherit the Holy Land with all its wealth and fertility. The blessing also was political—promising Jacob's superiority to his enemies. It bestowed the clan's leadership on Jacob.

Thus, we see that in patriarchal times the laying on of hands was a rite for conveying property and position within the extended family. In that ancient time there was no clear code of law. Therefore, one's sworn word was considered binding. This laying on of hands is one of the early roots of ordination to the Christian ministry.

In later years, as he neared death, Jacob would bless the sons of Joseph. (Gen. 48:8-22. Note verse 13 where he laid his hands on the boys.) We find no instances in the Old Testament of laying on hands to heal someone.

### Establishing a Relationship

As we have seen, in the Old Testament the oldest meaning of laying on hands was to bestow a blessing. This was usually accompanied with a prayer for prosperity. However, the most frequent use of the ritual was in the Hebrew sacrificial system. The worshiper or priest symbolically laid his hands on the sacrifice. This was a sign of dedicating it to the deity, or of transferring the worshiper's guilt to the animal.

Sacrificial worship in Israel was an act of worship of the one true God. It also represented an expression of the worshiper's devotion of himself to

God. In later Christian worship it was acknowledged that Christ alone is our sacrifice to God. It was by his death on the cross that true atonement was realized. Thus, the believer was admonished to offer his body to God as a living sacrifice. This is the essence of spiritual worship (Rom. 12:1).

The Old Testament ritual of laying hands on the victim did not represent some magical or mechanical tranference of one's sins. Rather, it was more a symbolic act of identification with the sacrifice. Thus, the worshiper became involved by his own devotion to God in what was done to the sacrifice. It represented his own surrender to God. By his obedience the worshiper enjoyed divine forgiveness and blessing.

To summarize the significance of laying on hands in sacrificial worship:

- The worshiper thus identified the offering as his own. He owned it and was sacrificing it to God.
- The worshiper presented the offering as a substitute for himself. The animal bore his guilt and paid his sin debt by dying—its blood was offered on the altar.
- The worshiper thus sought God's grace and forgiveness. Laying on hands was an outward sign of the person's inner intention. It was not simply a passive act of worship.

## Installing in an Office of Leadership

The closest parallel to ordination found in the Old Testament was Moses' transferral of his leadership on Joshua. In a public act the leader of the Hebrews conveyed his authority to his successor by laying hands on him in the presence of Eleazer the priest.

The Lord answered Moses, "Take Joshua son of Nun, a man endowed with spirit; lay your hand on him and set him before Eleazar the priest and all the community. Give him his commission in their presence, and delegate some of your authority to him, so that all the community of the Israelites may obey him. He must appear before Eleazar the priest, who will obtain a decision for him by consulting the Urim before the Lord; at his word they shall go out and shall come home, both Joshua and the whole community of the Israelites." Moses did as the Lord had commanded him. He took Joshua, presented him to Eleazar the priest and the whole community, laid his hands on him and gave him his commission, as the Lord had instructed him (Num. 27:18-23, NEB).

The commissioning of Joshua by Moses is similar to contemporary ordination practices in several ways:

1. The choice of Joshua was by God. He was divinely chosen. In ordination we expect the candidate to possess a divine call to the ministry. Moses' successor neither inherited the office, nor was he inducted by popular choice or vote. He was elected of God to lead the people according to God's will.

2. It grew out of a practical need. Moses prayed to God for someone to take up the leadership of the Israelites after him. Ordination grows out of the practical need for spiritual leaders within the church.

Concerning the laying on of hands in this passage, Alan Richardson writes: "An ordained ministry is thus consecrated to God's service and so is 'holy' and is at the time commissioned to act representatively by those who have laid on hands."[1] Obviously, this is what ordination has come to mean to Anglican Richardson, but it may be reading a bit too much into this ancient action. He points out that the Hebrew word for laying on hands (*samakh*) is literally translated "to lean upon" another. In this symbolic act Israel's guilt was transferred to the scapegoat. In the same way, Moses' spirit was transferred to Joshua. In later Hebrew history hands were laid on a rabbi at ordination symbolizing that the ordaining scholar was pouring his personality into his disciple.

3. Joshua was publicly set apart for his task of leadership. He now had Moses' authority. It was no private matter. He had hands laid on him in the presence of Eleazar and "all the community of the Israelites." He was commissioned for his new office by Moses. Ordination, likewise, is a public affair, not something done privately.

Wayne Ward contends that this passage exerted a profound influence on later Judaism. In the Jewish writings of the first century (the Mishnah) the rabbis cited this passage as the basis for the ordination of men into the rabbinate—by the laying on of hands. In all likelihood this later practice influenced Christian ordination. The church may have taken the idea of limiting those who lay on hands from Judaism. It appears that all the congregation once took part in the laying on of hands (see Num. 8:10 and Acts 6:6). This narrowing of participants may have come about as a practical matter—it would take a long time and prove awkward to have all the congregation lay on hands. Or it could have stemmed from the desire to vest authority in a "priestly class." Today in Baptist ordination practice, most often only fellow ordained ministers and perhaps deacons take part in the laying on of hands. Some churches are beginning to have the entire congregation participate.

## Laying on of Hands in the New Testament

In the new covenant this act is more closely related to ordination, but it had a wider significance as well. It was used in at least four ways:

### *Healing*

Jesus often healed the sick by laying his hands on the person.

A deaf mute's friends asked that Jesus lay his hand upon him (Mark 7:32). Jesus touched the man's ears and tongue, and his hearing and speech were restored.

Jesus laid his hands on a blind man in Bethsaida in Galilee, and his sight was restored (Mark 8:23-25).

Jesus healed a boy suffering with convulsions: "Jesus took him by the hand" (Mark 9:27).

A woman who had been stooped and crippled for eighteen years was healed by the Master: "And he laid his hands upon her, and immediately she was made straight, and she praised God" (Luke 13:13, RSV).

In Mark 5 we have the account of Jesus' raising the daughter of Jairus (lay president of a synagogue) from the dead. It was done by taking her by the hand (v. 41). Thus, he demonstrated faith's victory over death, and restored the child to her family.

There was healing in the Master's touch. "Now when the sun was setting, all those who had any that were sick with various diseases brought them to him; and he laid his hands on every one of them and healed them" (Luke 4:40, RSV). In this summary statement we see the significance of Jesus laying on his hands for healing.

This practice was also found in the New Testament church. The apostles healed the sick by the laying on of their hands.

Following Saul's encounter with the risen Christ en route to Damascus, he was struck blind. His sight was restored when Ananias laid hands on him (Acts 9:12,17). We have at least two accounts of the apostle Paul healing by the laying on of his hands. "And God did extraordinary miracles by the hands of Paul" (Acts 19:11, RSV). The father of Publius was seriously ill. "Paul visited him and prayed, and putting his hands on him healed him" (28:8, RSV).    In New Testament times, including the ministry of Jesus, laying on of hands was a sign which symbolized God's power becoming active in healing the sick. It was the means by which the power of God was effectively released. Not only Jesus, but the twelve and Paul exercised this power. This action was likely an influence on the later practice of laying on hands in ordination.

## Blessing

The laying on of hands was also a symbol of affection and blessings. In Mark 10:13-16 we have the lovely account of Jesus blessing the little children: "And they were bringing children to him, that he might touch them; and the disciples rebuked them. But when Jesus saw it he was indignant, and said to them, 'Let the children come to me, do not hinder them; for to such belongs the kingdom of God. Truly, I say to you, whoever does not receive the kingdom of God like a child shall not enter it.' And he took them in his arms and blessed them, laying his hands upon them" (RSV).

Jesus' blessing was different from Isaac's blessing Jacob. That represented the transference of an inheritance. Jesus' touch was an act of joy and love, and the children were blessed. Touching has great significance, even in ordination.

## At Baptism

The laying on of hands at baptism symbolized the bestowal of the Holy Spirit. It was a fairly prominent practice in the New Testament church.

Following the ascension of Christ, excited believers went everywhere sharing their resurrection faith. The gospel was taken even to Samaria, a place populated by Jews of mixed blood. Many there believed and symbolized their faith by being baptized. However, when Peter and John visited the new mission field, they found these believers had not yet received the gift of the Holy Spirit. "They had only been baptized in the name of the Lord Jesus. Then they laid their hands on them and they received the Holy Spirit" (Acts 8:16-17, RSV).

The missionary apostle Paul followed a similar practice later in Ephesus. "They were baptized in the name of the Lord Jesus. And when Paul had laid his hands upon them, the Holy Spirit came upon them; and they spoke with tongues and prophesied" (Acts 19:5-6, RSV).

Following the preaching of Peter, the Spirit "fell on all who heard the word." He also came upon Gentiles when there was no mention of any laying on of hands (see Acts 10:44-48).

Thus, we see that the laying on of hands often (but not always) followed the baptism of new believers. It symbolized the bestowal of the Holy Spirit.

## Empowered for Christian Ministry

We have an account of the selection of the first deacons (those who serve) in Acts 6. A problem in the Jerusalem church called for better organization. The congregation chose seven men to meet this need. The apostles decided: " 'Therefore, brethren, pick out from among you seven men of good repute, full of the Spirit and of wisdom, whom we may appoint to this duty. But we will devote ourselves to prayer and to the ministry of the word.' And what they said pleased the whole multitude, and they chose Stephen, a man full of faith and of the Holy Spirit, and Philip, and Prochorus, and Nicanor, and Timon, and Parmenas, and Nicolaus, a proselyte of Antioch. These they set before the apostles, and they prayed and laid their hands upon them" (Acts 6:3-6, RSV).

The text does not make it absolutely clear as to whether the entire congregation laid hands on the seven, or whether only the apostles did so. As we have seen in Numbers 8:10, the whole congregation of Israel laid hands on the Levites, setting them apart for service. This is likely the first account in the history of the New Testament church of the practice of ordination. In this simple rite early church leaders were consecrated to their practical ministry. Some would disagree that this was any kind of ordination.

If it was the apostles who laid hands on the seven, in all probability this was an action representing the congregation. This would have been a way of symbolizing the church's choice of these new leaders.

In Acts 13 we have another instance of the use of laying on of hands to designate men for a Christian ministry. If Acts 6 is the earliest account of the ordination of deacons, Acts 13 relates the ordination or commissioning of first-century missionaries. The church in Antioch, at the direction of the Holy Spirit, set apart Barnabas and Paul to their mission enterprize.

This was different from Ananias's laying hands on Paul after his conversion to cure his blindness. It was an ordination of the two men for a particular missionary endeavor. It was not ordination to a church office. The New Testament practice of ordination, if it is to be called that, was highly practical. It was not for the elevation of the ordinand but for the edification of the church and evangelistic outreach.

18

## Ordination to the Christian Ministry

Wayne Ward detects a deeper strain within the biblical evidence: the setting apart of a person to the vocation of Christian ministry. He summarizes the significance of the scriptural practice of laying on hands for Christian ministry:

1. "By laying on hands the people of God are invoking a divine blessing and symbolically bestowing a spiritual blessing upon the recipient.

2. "The 'people of Israel' or the 'whole congregation of believers' in the New Testament are, by this act, confirming the choice of certain 'spirit filled' persons to minister to them and in their behalf.

3. "By laying on hands the people were showing that something of themselves actually was transferred to the recipient: their personal concern, their ongoing prayers, their trust and support.

4. "The act sometimes demonstrated publically a succession of leadership (Moses to Joshua, Paul to Timothy).

5. "The coming of the Spirit in power, without the ritual of hands, reminds us that God is sovereign and free, choosing and empowering whomever he wills to be his ministers, unfettered by an ecclesiastical ritual of succession.

6. "Finally, laying on of hands may signify spiritual enduement for a particular Christian mission or activity, within a limited span of time, and without signifying a permanent ecclesiastical office."[2]

The practices of the early church were influenced by the synagogue. The leaders in this Jewish unit of worship were called elders (*presbuteroi* or presbyters). The church took over this title and office. We find Paul writing about ruling elders and preaching and teaching elders in 1 Timothy 5:17. The title "elder" dates back to the time of Moses (Ex. 18; 24).

There is little reason to believe that the New Testament church viewed its officers as a superior class of believers (clergy *vs.* laity). This was a distortion which came later in church history. The early church simply regarded its leaders as ministers of the congregation carrying out different functions within the one body of Christ (see 1 Cor. 12:12-31; Eph. 4:11-16).

Note that the initiative for ordination most often came at the leading of the Holy Spirit. We may be surprised today at some of the "unlikely candidates" whom God calls into the ministry. Occasionally, men are called and set apart almost against their will. George W. Truett is a prime example, as his biographer points out. It is not enough for an individual to feel called to the ministry. This call must also be confirmed by the action of a local congregation in Baptist practice.

Note that the ordination of Barnabas and Paul (or Saul, his Hebrew name) was preceded by a period of fasting and prayer. Then their setting apart was confirmed by the congregation. Baptist churches and ordination councils still ask for evidence of a divine call and set persons apart to the ministry with prayer and the laying on of hands. The act symbolizes the bestowal of divine blessings on the candidates and the assurance of the church's prayer support—the leader is not alone in his or her ministry.

Dr. Ward argues that "this is the biblical warrant for a continuing support and concern for the ordained minister by the ordaining church, throughout his ministry. It is also the basis of counsel, guidance, rebuke and even recall of the ordination if that drastic action should become necessary." This is a high ideal. However, in practice there is little follow-through after a person is ordained to the ministry by a local church. Most Baptist churches do not keep up with the persons and ministries of those whom they ordain. Many congregations would do well to give attention to this. Some could invite those whom they have ordained to return periodically to preach and renew the relationship with their ordaining church.

Based on the ordination of Barnabas and Paul in Acts 13, it could be argued that:

1. They were ordained for a particular missionary task, a given journey, and not for life.

2. Their ordination was limited to this specific need and did not set them apart as lifetime missionaries or ministers. Such a view might alter our concept of ordination. We generally take it to mean that a person is thereby set apart as a minister for life. Therefore, when one "leaves the ministry" (gives up a pastoral or preaching function), the church and the minister are usually at a loss as to what to do about his ordination. Ethically, the initiative should be taken by the minister to turn in his ordination certificate. Though he leaves any formal pattern of ministry, he can, of course, remain a "lay minister." This is a weakness in the Baptist practice of ordination and ministry. We have a loose denominational structure and individual congregations are not always sure what course of action is appropriate.

The New Testament pattern of ordination appears to be more functional than professional. It would play down any sharp and clear-cut distinction between the clergy and laity. We believe in the priesthood of all believers and the ministry of the laity, as well as the setting apart of called persons to specific ministries.

Ordination is official recognition by a local congregation and its sister churches that the Holy Spirit has called out certain persons to function in specialized ministry within the church and churches.

Within the New Testament the most highly developed view of ordination is found in the pastoral epistles (1 Tim.; 2 Tim.; Titus). Here we discover that a gift of God for ministry is recognized by ordination. "Do not neglect the gift you have, which was given you by prophetic utterance when the elders laid their hands upon you" (1 Tim. 4:14, RSV). Later, in a personal plea Paul admonishes Timothy to "Stir into flame the gift of God which is within you through the laying on of my hands" (2 Tim. 1:6, NEB).

Paul was in the group of elders who laid hands on the young minister, Timothy, at his ordination. There is no implication of any mechanical or magical conveying of grace in ordination—merely the reminder of spiritual gifts acknowledged in that symbolic act. Ordination was an outward confirmation of the inward call and obvious gifts of ministry already possessed by Timothy. Timothy and Titus were told by Paul to appoint elders or overseers (pastors or bishops) in the churches. This does not rule out congregational election of its leaders.

## Arguments in Favor of Ordination in the New Testament

The late H. E. Dana wrote helpfully about ordination. He argued that the church has set men apart as official leaders throughout Christian history. The roots of this practice are to be found in the Jewish synagogue and its ordination of rabbis.

While Jesus "ordained" the twelve apostles (Mark 3:14), the Greek word used does not mean there was a service of recognition. Rather, it designated these men for a type of service. It was more the designation of a function than the creation of an office. The origin of Christian ordination is likely the setting apart of the seven to serve the church and assist the apostles in the Jerusalem church (Acts 6).

Baptists want to base their practices, including ordination, on the New Testament pattern. However, the evidence there is admittedly meager. The word ordain (kathistemi) is used of church officers only twice (Acts

6:3; Titus 1:5). No real details are given as to the procedure of ordination in the New Testament church. We have no description of the ordination ceremony in the New Testament. However, we do discern such elements as:

1. One's divine call at the initiative of the Holy Spirit.
2. Congregation concurrence or election.
3. A time of prayer and consecration.
4. The laying on of hands by the apostles or elders and likely by the entire congregation.

Dana wrote, "When we look into these passages (Acts 6:6; 13:3; 1 Tim. 4:14; 5:22; and 2 Tim. 1:6 where laying on of hands is mentioned in a ceremonial sense), we are convinced that ordination was a public and formal act employed for the setting apart of those whom God had called to tasks of Christian leadership. We may be perfectly sure that ordination as a ceremony of installation originated in apostolic times."[3]

While Barnabas and Paul were set apart for their first missionary journey, Timothy appears to have received a more general ordination to the gospel ministry (see 1 Tim. 4:14; 2 Tim. 1:6; Acts 16:1-3). Paul's admonition, "lay hands hastily on no man" (1 Tim. 5:22, ASV) obviously refers to the ordination of elders or pastors. There are seventeen references to this office in the New Testament. The elder's function in the church was basically twofold: administration and teaching or preaching (see 1 Tim. 5:17). There is no reason to suppose that ordination limited a person to service in a single congregation. It must have been more a setting apart to the ministry of the churches, or the church as a whole. Ordination should qualify or recognize a person for service throughout the kingdom.

The pattern for Christian ministry is the ministry of Christ. While his coming, calling, and ministry were unique and once for all, still it has become the pattern for our ministry. Jesus was self-giving, not self-serving, a "man for others." That is the modern minister's goal.

Jesus set the example and taught that he who would be greatest should be the servant of all. The minister, like his Master, is to be more a servant than an ecclesiastical professional. Jesus took the world's standard of greatness (ancient and modern) and stood it on its head (Mark 10:45).

Jesus exemplified the Father's character by loving even his enemies. The minister is called to be a caring and helping person. Jesus called himself the Good Shepherd. It is noteworthy that the English word *pastor* comes from a Latin root which means "shepherd." See Peter's admonition to his fellow pastors (1 Pet. 5:1-4).

Jesus' role was that of prophet, priest, and king. The minister has the dual ministry: as prophetic preacher he is to declare the whole counsel of God; as a pastor he is to "comfort . . . my people" (Isa. 40:1).

We understand the laying on of hands in ordination to have the following significance.

1. It conveys no special status, rights, or authority. It creates no clergy class and does not elevate the minister to a superior position within the family of God.

2. It involves a recognition of divine call to the gospel ministry and the possession of the gifts of ministry.

3. It is a public commissioning to the responsibilities and functions of a specialized ministry within the church. He or she becomes a "playing coach" with an enabling ministry. "And his gifts were that some should be apostles, some prophets, some evangelists, some pastors and teachers, for the equipment of the saints, for the work of ministry, for building up the body of Christ" (Eph. 4:11-12, RSV).

4. It is an act of consecration to the call and task. Ordination is a high honor, but it is much more. It is a total commitment to do the Father's will in a particular ministry within the church. The role may change with the passing of time, the person's maturing, and changing needs within the life of the church, but the call and the commitment are constant.

## Arguments Against Ordination in the New Testament

Some scholars have argued that there is no warrant within the New Testament for ordination. While the Protestant Reformation stripped the Christian ministry of its sacramental priestly character, still it kept a simple form of ordination.

Eduard Schweizer raises his objection to biblical precedent for ordination by writing, "Fundamentally the New Testament knows no distinction between ministry and office."[4] He feels that the titles given were "purely functional terms" more related to gifts than official positions within the church. He contends that Paul knows nothing of ordination as a rite of installation to a particular ministry. He does not consider the pastoral epistles to be Pauline, and there, as elsewhere in the New Testament, he sees the laying on of hands as an act of healing, blessing, or accompanying baptism.

23

Schweizer argues that the laying on of hands upon Barnabas and Paul in Acts 13 is "not a matter of ordination" but an assignment to service. He views this and the similar experience of the seven in Acts 6 as the receiving of a blessing. He questions whether the laying on of hands in 1 and 2 Timothy is ordination at all. He says it could refer to the time of their baptism when the Holy Spirit was imparted. He argues that it is not the matter of the candidate's preparation nor the apostle's authority but the "event of God's Spirit that qualifies a person to serve."

While Schweizer's emphasis on the importance and role of the Spirit in the ministry is welcome, his insistence that there is no ordination to the ministry in the New Testament period seems strained.

Another scholar who has raised serious question about the evidence of ordination in the New Testament is Heber F. Peacock. He defines ordination as, "The initial rite which sets aside an individual to the Christian ministry."[5] He concedes that it is an almost universal practice within the church. However, he writes, "There is a real question as to whether ordination actually appears in the New Testament. It is only in the book of Acts and in the pastoral epistles that passages are found which can with any degree of certainty be made to refer to ordination." I've always felt this type argument to be weak. It is used against such doctrines as the virgin birth. How many times does the Holy Spirit have to speak in Scripture for us to take him seriously?

Peacock feels that a sharp distinction should be made between the laying on of hands and ordination. The former does have broader uses, as we have seen, such as blessing, healing, and in connection with baptism. Peacock says that Paul's admonition to Timothy in 1 Timothy 4:14 may refer to his baptism and not to ordination. (But did a presbytery lay hands on Timothy as a newly baptized convert?) He contends the same for 2 Timothy 1:6. "Rekindle the gift of God that is within you through the laying on of my hands" (RSV). (Did Paul baptize Timothy?) He raises the same question in reference to 1 Timothy 5:22, "Lay hands hastily on no one" (ASV).

In his article, Peacock writes that scholars claim Christian ordination was modeled on the pattern of the ordination of a Jewish rabbi. He questions this, saying this would have meant an official ministry with apostolic succession. Peacock rather sees the ministry in the New Testament church as charismatic and functional. Certainly he is correct in this description of the New Testament ministry. However, it does not follow that the church was not influenced by Jewish ordination practices. The church took over the pattern of synagogue worship, for example, but poured Christian content into it. While ordination gave the rabbi official status and authority, it does not automatically follow that ordination to the Christian ministry did the same.

Peacock argues convincingly that, "The background of New Testament ordination is not the transfer of . . . authority from one person to another; it is the prayer-blessing concept of laying on hands seen in healing, blessings, and the gift of the Spirit." He sees a spiritual significance in the laying on of hands at ordination. It is a "prayer for the continued presence and blessing of the Spirit." He sees the ministry as the direct gift of the Holy Spirit to the church and to the individual. Therefore, he views the laying on of hands as an act of "intercession."

Ordination conveys no new rights, privileges, or authority. But it is a symbol of the acceptance of new responsibilities from the Holy Spirit on behalf of the church.

## Conclusion

It may be argued that there is no evidence of ordination in the New Testament. I would concede that the evidence found there is sparse and fragmentary. However, there are enough indications to conlude that the roots of ordination are to be found in the practice of the first-century church.

This simple Spirit-led setting apart of church leaders was formalized in later church history and even distorted into a superior clergy class. However, that is not ample reason to reject ordination or to deny that it was present, even embryonically in the early church. All forms of church organization were seminal then, but the beginnings were there—including ordination to the gospel ministry by which men were set apart for service within the church.

[1]*Theology of the New Testament* (New York: Harper & Bros., 1958), p. 329.

[2]*Baptist Standard,* Oct. 18, 1978.

[3]*Baptist Program,* April, 1970, p. 8.

[4]"Church Order in the New Testament," *Studies in Biblical Theology,* No. 32 (London: SCM Press, 1961), pp. 206-207.

[5]*Review & Expositor,* vol. 55, no. 3, p. 262-271.

# 2.
# Ordination in the History of the Church

Life in the first-century church was highly spontaneous and unstructured. It also was pulsating with excitement. Jesus set up very little, if any, organization prior to his death. He left it to the apostles to share the gospel good news—and share it they did!

The church arose out of an overwhelming belief that Jesus was alive again, raised from the dead by the power of God. He appeared to more than 500 believers prior to his ascension. He appeared to those who loved him. They were filled with joy and happily shared their faith in the risen Christ even at great personal cost, including martyrdom. (It is noteworthy that our English word *martyr* is almost a transliteration of the Greek word for "witness.")

First-century Christians were convinced that the kingdom or rule of God announced by John the Baptist had dawned in the Christ-event. And they went everyplace announcing the gospel of the kingdom. The resurrection turned the cross into a sign of triumph, and the Easter faith was born. "He is alive!"

The new faith spread like a forest fire into the surrounding religiously bankrupt world. Historians marvel at the rapid expansion of Christianity. Many Gentile "God-fearers" sympathetic to Judaism were won to faith in Jesus as the Messiah. This new faith gave meaning and purpose to life and death. One of the strongest arguments that ours is a resurrection faith is the establishment of the Lord's Day as a time of Christian worship.

The spontaneity of New Testament faith did not call for complicated organization. It was a movement which flowed at the direction of the Holy Spirit. There were hundreds of eyewitnesses fresh from their contacts with Jesus. Outstanding within this group were the twelve who had spent three years being taught by the Master.

27

There was an amazing spiritual equality within the early church. Women were accorded privileges we are arguing about nineteen centuries later—Phoebe was a deaconess, and Philip's daughters were prophets or inspired preachers. There also was amazing equality between classes. Most early Christians were doubtless slaves. Yet "in Christ" there was no bond or free, Jew or Gentile, male or female. The church appears to have functioned in fact as a spiritual democracy. Decisions were made by the congregation under the lordship of Christ at the Spirit's leading.

While the apostles and other church leaders were respected and honored, their positions were not those of privilege. Paul dared to disagree with Peter, "Chief of the Apostles," and James, the Lord's half-brother, in the famous Jerusalem church conference. And Paul's position was correct—admitting Gentiles fully to the faith, without requiring their observance of certain Jewish rituals.

As long as the eyewitnesses, including the apostles, were alive, there was little need for much organization within the church, nor even for Christian Scriptures. Who wants to read a book when he can hear or interview an eyewitness? All this began to change with the death of the eyewitnesses and the coming to leadership of second generation believers. Then the writings and reminiscences of the eyewitnesses began to take on a special importance to the church. Mark's Gospel is believed to be based on the preaching of Simon Peter. With the passing of the apostolic generation the New Testament writings came to be accepted as the continuing apostolic witness.

Time passed and the faith spread from Palestine into the pagan Roman Empire, and a different situation developed. Churches planted in city-centers by missionaries like Paul, Barnabas, and Silas required leadership once their founders moved on. This need resulted in the production of much of the corpus of our New Testament. Leaders were also elected or appointed to train new converts and reach out to still others.

There seems to be an ambiguous pattern to this leadership. There was little uniformity such as the "three-fold ministry of bishops, elders, and deacons" claimed by many. Even titles were applied rather haphazardly to similar functions. Pastors were called elders or presbyters and bishops or overseers. They were charged with both teaching or preaching and ruling (administration).

As the eyewitnesses passed off the scene and their witness became crystallized in the New Testament documents, the church's ministry also became more formalized. This was necessary to counter the rise of doctrinal heresies within the churches.

The organizational patterns, as well as style of worship, in the early church were influenced by the Jewish synagogue. Another influence in church doctrinal statements was Greek thought and philosophy. As the church became increasingly made up of Gentiles, it also took on some of the organizational patterns of the Roman government. The New Testament ideal of the ministry is that of servants rather than "princes of the church." The form of church government which appears most consonant with the New Testament is congregational—a spiritual democracy beneath of lordship of Christ. Ministers and deacons are spiritual leaders but not dictators or rulers. The authority for decision-making rests with the congregation.

## In the First Century

All Christian ministry had its origin in the ministry of Christ, who came not to be ministered to but to minister (Mark 10:45). He fulfilled the priestly ministry of the Old Covenant and became the great High Priest of the New (Heb. 7:11 ff). Christ himself was commissioned by the Father for his mission on earth (John 20:21).

The New Testament material shows progression from a simple and casual toward more structured forms of ministry. These documents appear to show no distinction between the clergy and laity. All were considered ministers. There is no single pattern of ministry and church government within the New Testament. That is why various churches find evidence there for episcopal, presbyterian, and congregational forms of government. Uniform patterns of church government and ministry developed later in the second century of Christian history. Basic forms of ministry in the first-century church were fourfold:

1. The twelve, Jesus' original disciples.
2. Apostles, including the twelve but also including others who were "sent," such as the apostle Paul.
3. Prophets and teachers. In the New Testament the term prophet was used as a title for inspired preachers.
4. Other Christian leaders such as deacons. It does not appear that deacons were a junior rank within the clergy in the early church.

The basic pattern of ministry was the priesthood of all believers, and each Christian had his or her own particular ministry according to the gifts

29

of the Holy Spirit. See such passages as 1 Corinthians 12 and Ephesians 4:11 ff.

*The twelve* had a unique significance in the church because they had been called and trained by Jesus himself. They shared with their Master in the ongoing ministry of the people of God (see Luke 22:30; Rev. 21:14).

*The apostles.* This title was applied to early missionaries including Paul (see Rom. 16:7; 1 Cor. 15:5,7). The apostles spread the faith and conserved the words and works of Jesus within the early church.

*Prophets and teachers* were major gifts to the Christian community by the Holy Spirit (1 Cor. 12:28). They were not so much elected by the church as called out by the Holy Spirit. They gave expression to and interpreted the doctrines of the Christian faith. It appears that the focus of the preacher's ministry was the unsaved. And the teacher's task was the instruction of new converts.

*Bishops and elders* were local church leaders. See 1 Peter 5:1; James 5:14; and Acts 11:30 for references to elders *(presbuteroi)*. Bishops or overseers *(episkopoi)* are cited in Acts 20:17,28; Philippians 1:1; and Titus 1:5 ff. Deacons *(diakonoi)* are referred in Philippians 1:1 and 1 Timothy 3:1,8 ff. These three offices refer to ministry functions within the life of the church of the New Testament period. Elders have parallels in the Judaism of the period. Scholars generally agree that within the New Testament the terms bishop and elder do not refer to two different levels of ministry. They were both used to describe the pastoral role—shepherds of the flock.

Interestingly, within the New Testament Christian ministers were not called priests. The reason for this is that the whole church constituted a priesthood (1 Pet. 2:9). Christians as a whole were designated as "kings and priests" (Rev. 1:6). Christ alone fulfilled the priestly offices of the Old Covenant as our High Priest opening up the way to the Father.

Ministers or pastors functioned as shepherds, caring for the people of God and preserving unity within the church (1 Cor. 12). In the pastoral epistles the guarding of right doctrine was also a primary function of the ministry. Ministers were designated and set apart to their task by the laying on of hands. The verb "ordain" may be defined as a "voting by stretching out one's hands." Ordination was a public recognition of one's having and exercising the gifts of the ministry (1 Tim. 4:14).

While the pastoral epistles regard one of the functions of ministers to be the transmission of sound doctrine, there is no mention of any kind of "apostolic succession." That was a later development in the history of the church.

## Ordination in the Second Century

As the church continued to grow, its ministry and organization became more formal. This pattern is also discernable within the development of doctrine and worship. As an example, William Barclay has argued that the observance of the Lord's Supper moved from the home to the church, from an actual meal to a symbolic meal, and from a simple observance to an elaborate one. Its simple symbolism became an ornate sacrament with the passing of time.

The most prominent development in ministry within the second century was the emergence of the ruling bishop. By the middle of the century the principal leadership in the church became the monarchical episcopate. The bishop was a symbol of both unity and doctrinal purity. He presided over the elders or pastors and was assisted by deacons. An order or ranking within the ministry appeared: bishops, elders, and deacons. This was a departure from or adding to the New Testament pattern. It was occasioned by the rise of heresies such as gnostic influence in the church.

The churches felt a need for authority to protect them and define correct doctrine. That authority was vested in the bishop. This led to the concept of the bishops being in succession from the apostles. Along with the rise of bishops to power came an increase in the use of the language of priesthood within the church. A hierarchy was also in the process of development.

The ordination service, while still basically prayer and the laying on of hands, became more elaborate. It still required the vote or approval of the congregation to ordain a man. The presence and participation of a bishop at ordination symbolized the unity of the whole church in the act. Thus, the bishop had a growing significance in the rite. In the second-century *Acts of Peter* the apostles were described as "those on whom Christ had imposed his hands."

Ordination to the ministry was still considered the work of the Holy Spirit. However, the bishop's approval and official endorsement of the candidate became increasingly important. It was finally concluded that only the bishop had the authority to ordain and designate who would perform pastoral functions within the church.

Ignatius (AD 112) wrote, "Let that be considered a valid Eucharist over which the bishop presides, or the one to whom he commits it. Wherever the bishop appears there let the people be, just as, wherever Christ Jesus is, there is the Catholic Church. It is not permitted either to baptize or to hold a love-feast apart from the bishop."[1]

"The Apostolic Tradition" is the earliest surviving account of an ordination service. It became a model for ordination in the Roman church into the third century. Candidates for ordination first had to be approved by the church as a whole. A prayer was offered for the ordinand during which he received the laying on of hands. The contents of the ordination prayer was largely drawn from Scripture. Even though this was a time of persecution in the history of the church, the prayer reflected a confident faith and hope in God.

When a bishop was chosen, his election was confirmed by the congregation along with elders or pastors and the bishops of other communities. Other bishops present at the ordination would take part in the consecration service. They laid hands on the candidate while presbyters and people prayed for the descent of the Holy Spirit.

Within the next century the bishop acquired the functions of governing the church. The consecration of bishops came to have a threefold significance:

1. His acceptance by the people of his local community was an essential part of his ordination. This bishop first had to be tested or proven by the local church. In ordination, therefore, he was bound to the local congregation and they to him for the exercising of his gift of ministry.

2. The concern and recognition of the church as a whole were expressed in the presence of neighboring bishops who came to show that what was happening was not simply of local significance. The bishop's office, therefore, was seen as one of the links which bound the local church to the entire church as the body of Christ.

3. The bishop was seen as having a particular status in relation to the activity of the Holy Spirit working in the church. The church was still under the influence of the Spirit. The ordination prayer was a prayer for an outpouring of the Holy Spirit in connection with the laying on of hands. A presbyter or pastor would be ordained by the bishop laying his hands on his head with the other presbyters present also touching him.

The deacon was ordained by the bishop alone. The function of deacons was not so much a priestly function as a helper or assistant to the bishop. They looked after church property and answered to the bishop. Widows and readers were appointed but not ordained. Healers were not ordained since this was considered a charismatic gift. Biblical materials, both from the Old and New Testaments, were used in the ordination prayers.

It is interesting that between AD 200 and 400 the church made a great deal of typology. Moses and his helpers became an organizational pattern for the priesthood.

Enthroning a bishop was the one act which distinguished the bishop's ordination from that of a presbyter or pastor. His throne was called a "cathedra" from which we get the word cathedral. To speak "ex cathedra" is to make an official proclamation. The bench for priests were on either side of the bishop's chair. Tertullian wrote, "The difference between the ordained and the people is established by church authority and by the sacred rite of admission to where the priests sit in the church." Honor was thus paid to those who were ordained by according them the chief seats.

The imposition of the "Gospel-book" was an interesting innovation at ordination. At the close of the fourth century this rite was established. At the consecration of a bishop the Gospels were placed on the nape of his neck and held by two assistants while hands were being laid on him. Thus, he was ordained beneath the Gospels.

The pagans of the early Christian centuries used a word *cheirotonein* which meant to elect by show of hands. This word was used in the writings of Ignatius for appointing a deacon or a bishop. A similar word—*cheirepithesia*—was used within the Christian context for the laying on of hands in order to make a man a bishop. Chrysostom wrote, "The man's hand is imposed, but God does all. In fact, it is his hand which touches the head of the one being ordained when he is rightly ordained."

## A Theology of Priesthood

In 2 Corinthians 5:18-20 the apostles are said to have carried out their ministry on behalf of Christ, beseeching man to be reconciled to God. Chrysostom commented on these verses: "On behalf of Christ meant in place of Christ." "The words at the imposition of hands are sacramental and by them the elected one is sealed for his task and receives authority that emboldens him to offer sacrifice to God in the place of Christ" (Ambrosiaster's commentary on 1 Tim. 4:14).

The concept of the Christian priesthood was built on Old Testament types and models. There were very few references to the New Testament. The consecration prayer for the bishop was based on God's relationship with Moses and the significance of the priestly vestments in relation to the Aaronic priesthood. A contrast was made between the "vestments of the flesh" of the Aaronic priesthood and the "vestments of the spirit" in ordination to the Christian priesthood. Thus, we find the development of a priesthood within the Christian church based on a priestly hierarchy. The idea of succession came from the Old Testament idea of priesthood as well. This seems ironic since our faith is based principally on the New Testament documents.

The bishop of Rome consecrated other bishops from his own province. They would be elected by the Christians in a given locality with the bishop's election being confirmed by the bishop of Rome. The bishop of Rome always would consecrate the new bishop on a Sunday. He would recite the ordination prayer over the candidate and then embrace him. The newly ordained bishop would then join the other bishops present at the service. The authority of the bishop of Rome was extended agressively as he came to be viewed as Peter's successor and *pontifex maximus* or the highest priest within the church.

The ordination of a pope was slightly different from the ordination of a bishop. Before the ninth century, the pope would always be selected from among the deacons of the Roman church and never from among the bishops. He would put on the liturgical vestments and prostrate himself before the altar. Three ordination prayers were recited and the deacons held an open Gospel-book above the candidate's head. The book symbolized the biblical authority of the Christ-event. Then the pope would take his throne and begin singing *Gloria in Excelsis.*

In the early Roman rites of ordination, the people played a very definite part in the election of candidates. However, with the move toward centralization of authority this began to change. Thus, they began to take a lesser role than in the third century and earlier. The people stood and prayed in silence. Finally, the ordination prayers lost much of their simplicity and directness. They came to be based more on the Old Testament than on the New as they had been earlier.

## Ordination in the Eastern Church

The Byzantine church recognized five orders of ordained ministers. The three major orders were bishop, presbyter, and deacon. But there were two suborders of subdeacon and elector, also known as canter and psalmist. There were also candlebearers and deaconesses. All were ordained by the laying on of hands and prayer. The common prayer was this: "The divine grace, which always brings healing to what is weak and supplies what is lacking, ordains the devout priest to be priest of his church. Let us pray therefore that the grace of the Holy Spirit may come upon him."

At the ordination of a bishop, the candidate was led before the consecrating bishop, who was seated, and presented to the people. The consecrating bishop would then ask him why he had come.

He would reply: "For the laying on of hands for the grace of the episcopal office, because the clergy have elected."

He was brought closer to the bishop who asked him to profess his faith. He then would recite the Nicene Creed. The candidate would affirm his orthodoxy. He declared his faith in the doctrines of the Trinity, the incarnation, and the Word of God. He then repudiated all heresies.

The candidate was invested with the robes of his office and given the pastoral staff "to guide, protect, and to chasten." He was taken into the sanctuary where he knelt before the altar with his arms crossed before him and his head bowed at the communion table. The open book of the Gospels was placed on his shoulders, being held in place by the two other bishops. The principal bishop would recite three prayers, praying that the candidate would receive the grace of the Holy Spirit for the work of bishop. He also prayed that he might follow the example of the Good Shepherd who gave his life for the sheep. The candidate and those who ordained him would exchange the kiss of peace. The newly ordained man would be enthroned and would give the blessing by reading from the Epistles. He was then the first to receive communion and to distribute it to his fellow priests and others who were present.

The Eastern Orthodox view is that a bishop must be assigned to a local church in order to be a bishop. He is not a "bishop at large." They also believe that a man is not a valid priest unless he is connected to a particular church. This was the view within the Western church until around AD 1200. However, Roman Catholics now teach the concept that ordination bestows the episcopal or priestly office even if the man is not assigned to a local church, or even if he leaves the ministry. This view is foreign to the understanding of the Eastern Orthodox Church. They reject "absolute ordination." A statement dating from 1140 declares: "We decree that no person ought to be ordained in an absolute manner, neither priest, nor deacon, nor any cleric." The man ordained has to be attached to a local congregation.

Vogel contends that the acceptance of absolute ordination arose from the practice of celebrating the Eucharist in "private Masses" and accepting a gift for doing so. Thus, the wealthy could have private chaplains who were not pastors of a church.

The Eastern Orthodox Church teaches that there are two essential aspects in ordination: the laying on of hands and the assignment of a candidate to be connected with a specific local congregation. They do not speak of the universal church apart from local churches.

## Ordination in Medieval Times

North of the Alps before AD 950 the rite of ordination developed in a way unknown at Rome. Spanish and Irish traditions would later be incorporated into the traditions of the Roman Church. This composite rite and its elaboration became popular by the time of the Middle Ages.

The candidate was presented to the people on a Wednesday and Friday before his ordination on Sunday. The candidate came before the congregation at the beginning of the ordination service. A message was read requesting the people's approval for the one about to be ordained. The people would respond by saying, "He is worthy." Then there followed a bidding prayer and the ordination prayer. The import of the prayer was that the candidate might live up to the responsibilities of his office. Hands were placed on his head. When several men were ordained at one time, prayers were offered collectively.

During the Middle Ages, the services of ordination were enriched with many additional prayers and ceremonies. These varied from one location to another. The principal new addition was anointing the candidate.

When a bishop was ordained, he was enthroned and given the episcopal staff called the *cambuta,* a word of Celtic Latin origin. In earlier times deacons were assistants to the bishops and new bishops were ordained from among the deacons. Now the deacons became a rank within the priesthood.

Under the influence of a mystical thrust, the Roman church began to designate seven orders or ranks within the ministry. All of these were seen as extensions of the life of Christ on earth. This elaborate explanation was given: "He was doorkeeper when he opened the door of the ark and closed it again. He was gravedigger when he called forth Lazarus from the tomb. He was lector when he opened the book of Isaiah in the midst of the synagogue.... He was subdeacon when he poured water in a basin and washed the disciples' feet. He was deacon when he blest the chalice and gave it to the apostles to drink. He was priest when he blest the bread and gave it likewise to them. He was bishop when he taught the people in the temple." The idea was that every order within the ministry was a participation in the work of Christ.

The earliest reference to anointing at ordination comes from Roman Britain. It is thought that the idea had its origin, however, among Coptic Christians in Egypt. It spread by way of trade routes through Spain to Ireland, England, and Wales. The minister's hands were anointed as part of the ordination service.

There was an obvious parallel between the anointing of kings in Spain and of the Scottish kings on Iona around 700 and the anointing of a bishop. The bishop was usually anointed on his head while the hands of the priest were anointed. The prayer was given: "Thou didst give command to thy servant Moses that he should establish Aaron, his brother, as priest by the pouring of this oil after he had been washed in water." The idea of anointing at ordination may have been a carry-over from feudalism.

Symbols of ordination were given to the candidate. A book was given to the lector; a candle to the acolyte; keys to the doorkeeper. The king was crowned in much the same way as the bishop who was considered a prince of the church. All this elaborateness of ordination was given a biblical basis. That must have required considerable imagination.

The Irish claimed that Christ acted as a bishop when he blessed the apostles at the time of his ascension. "Everyone knows the Savior appointed the bishops to the churches, for before he ascended into the heavens he laid hands on the apostles and ordained them bishops."

The elaborateness of the ordination service was parallel to the great emphasis on the sacramental role of ministers. Jerome wrote of those who "with hallowed lips make the Body of Christ." The idea was that when the priest said the magical words over the elements of the Lord's Supper, they became the literal body and blood of Christ.

The Council of Trent in 1563 asserted the doctrine that sacramental character was conferred in the act of ordination. The hierarchy in the church was said to be of divine origin and consisted of bishops, presbyters, and deacons.

In the modern Roman Catholic Church the candidate receives the symbols of his office including the Gospel-book, a ring, and the pastoral staff. And in the case of a bishop, the presiding bishop or archbishop puts the miter on the candidate's head as well.

## The Reformation Churches and Ordination

Medieval theology and practice of ordination were questioned by the reformers. They rejected the hierarchical structure of the medieval ministry with its seven orders of ministers. They also rejected the concept of a sacrificial priesthood able to consecrate the body and blood of Christ as being contrary to the teaching of the New Testament. The reformers tried to restore a pure ministry of "the Word and sacrament" within the life and worship of the church.

Robert G. Torbet contends that the Protestant Reformation did not so much "unfrock the clergy as it ordained the laity."[2] This is a helpful insight into the shift of emphasis in the reformed churches. There was a reaction against highly institutionalized Christianity with its rigid lines of demarcation between priests and people. Also, there was an elevation of the importance of lay ministry within the body of Christ.

Some of the reformed churches kept the office of bishop but did not see it as constituting a separate or superior order to that of other ministers. The bishop simply had a more functional assignment. In some of the churches the office of deacon was retained. Their function was to care for the needy. The reformers did not believe that ordination conferred special grace upon the candidate or that it gave him an indelible character.

Medieval ordination rites had grown very elaborate. The reformers tried to return to the very simple and basic elements found in the New Testament itself. Most of the reformed churches came to the following conclusions.

1. The ordination would include an examination of beliefs, morality, and the sincerity of the candidate's call to the ministry. There was usually some form of electing the person to be a minister or at least of ratifying the choice of the candidate by the entire church at the time of his ordination. The candidate would give a public declaration of his faith and his call. Usually this was in the form of a series of questions and answers in the public ordination service.

2. Preparation for ordination on the part of the candidate was usually

in the form of prayer and fasting. It was a time for spiritual self-examination.

3. Ordination was carried out within the regular Sunday morning worship service. It was accompanied by preaching. The sermon would emphasize the duties of the minister and the congregation.

4. There would be an ordination prayer by both the congregation and the minister who was presiding or in charge. The act of ordination itself was performed by the laying on of hands. This varied from one reformed church to another. In some it was done by other ordained ministers who were present. In others it was done by ordained ministers and representatives of the laity. In some services all the ordained persons present would take part in the laying on of hands. In others all believers present would take part.

### Lutheran Ordination

Martin Luther could find no evidence in the New Testament for the office of bishop distinct from that of presbyter or pastor. Lutheran churches in Sweden, however, kept the idea of the historic succession of bishops. In Denmark the office of the bishop was kept without any idea of spiritual or historic succession. In Germany the title of bishop was abolished altogether.

A bishop was not regarded as having any power to ordain but rather received his authority from the church. Luther believed that every Christian was a priest before God with the duty of sharing the faith with those about him by proclaiming and teaching the Word of God. Therefore, ordination simply bestowed the functions of public preaching and the administration of the sacraments on those who were chosen to be ministers. The priesthood belonged to the church as a whole.

Luther wrote an ordination service in 1535 which became the basis of the services of most of the Lutheran churches. Its features included:

1. Prayer by the congregation for the candidate, usually in the form of a litany or a hymn.

2. An address by the presiding minister on the duties and obligations of ministers followed by a series of questions put to the candidate.

3. The laying on of hands by the presiding minister and other ministers accompanied by a repeating of the Lord's Prayer and an ordination prayer. The ordination was usually concluded with a hymn and the

observance of the Lord's Supper or Eucharist followed. The bishop's ordination, where there were bishops in Lutheran churches, was similar but more elaborate.

## Ordination in the Reformed Churches

The reformed churches usually identify four ministerial officers: pastor, teacher, elder, and deacon. These were found in the New Testament, but only the first three were strictly ministers of the Word—pastors, teachers, and elders. John Calvin was the reformed church leader in Geneva. When a new minister was needed, other ministers selected and examined a suitable candidate. If approved, he was submitted to the city council for their approval and finally to the people. Geneva was a city-state and a theocracy. A period of probation was then delcared. During this time, inquiries were made about the character and faith of the candidate, and any objection to his ordination could be entered. If nothing was discovered to discredit him, he would be formally elected by the people and set apart with prayer by other ministers. Calvin omitted the laying on of hands because of the superstitions which he felt clung to the practice.

In Scotland the procedure used in Geneva was adopted at first, and there was no laying on of hands. John Knox substituted the giving of "the right hand of fellowship" for the laying on of hands. Later, however, laying on of hands was introduced in the ordination of ministers under pressure from King James VI.

In 1636 the king tried to impose the Anglican ordination rites on the cots but with little success. The Presbyterian form of church government was adopted in the north.

In 1645 the Westminster Assembly gave directions for the ordination of a minister. The candidate was to be examined by other ministers. But the consent of the congregation was still necessary for his ordination. A sermon was given outlining the duties of the minister and the responsibilities of the congregation. Questions were put to the candidate and to the congregation. Then the ministers who were present laid hands upon the candidate while the ordination prayer was given. This was followed with a charge to the minister and the people and a prayer commending him to God. The service was concluded with the psalm and the pronouncement of a blessing or benediction.

This is basically the form of ordination by the church of Scotland. However, at the conclusion of the service the Lord's Prayer is repeated by the congregation, and the moderator declares the candidate to be ordained. All the ministers present give him the right hand of fellowship. The congregation declares their support for him, and the rite is concluded with prayer, singing, and a blessing.

## Ordination in the Anglican Church

The first published ordination service for bishops, priests, and deacons which appeared in the Church of England dates from 1550. The services were very similar except that the bishop's ordination was carried out a little more "solemnly and at greater length." The ordination of deacons was considerably simplified. Ordination admitted ministers to the church with public prayer and laying on of hands.

In discussing the Anglican view of ordination, Alan Richardson states that "it appears likely the original apostles ordained persons to the pastoral ministry." He sees this as conveying the grace of God and a gift of the Holy Spirit. Christ as head of the church acts through his body at the ordination of a minister and at the baptism of a layman. Both these "acts of Christ in his church are signified by the laying on of hands." And both actions are accompanied by the gift of the Holy Spirit.

Richardson also argues for authentic apostolic succession through ordination. Irenaeus, in his book against heresies (*Libros Quinque Adversus Haereses*), claimed to be able to give the names of the bishops appointed by the apostles in the different churches, along with the names of their successors down to his own day (around AD 180). Richardson does note, however, that the New Testament itself mentions mothing about a succession from the apostles. The only occasion in the New Testament where the word for succession occurs is in Acts 24:27. There Festus is called the successor of Felix—both secular rulers.

This Anglican scholar states his case for apostolic succession symbolized by the laying on of hands:

The impressive thing about the chain of laying on of hands, down all the centuries and across all continents, is that it is a *fact*, not a problem that requires explaining by a theory. It is a fact which testifies to the Gospel of Jesus Christ, that he is come in the flesh, and that he has gathered the elect into one Church, one body. The Gospel is not a series of "spiritual" truths; it is the proclamation of a redemption in history, in the flesh of Jesus Christ, in his actual, visible tangible body (1

41

Jn. 1:1; 4:2), his body which is still actual, visible and tangible, upon which hands have been literally, even materialistically, laid. The succession by the laying on of hands is the sign and instrument of the unity of the church, which is not an "ideal" Church, a "spiritual" body merely, but a real body that can be seen in the bodies of those on whom hands have been laid. The laying on of hands in baptism and in ordination is the Church's witness in every century that Jesus Christ is come in the flesh. Docetism in every age seeks a "spiritual" Gospel, because it cannot believe that God can or will tabernacle in humanity, in real, flesh-and-blood men and women with bodies as well as souls to be saved.[3]

There are now 65,000,000 Anglicans in the world, including 3,000,000 Episcopalians in the United States. Their spiritual leader is the Archbishop of Canterbury.

At ordination the candidates were given symbols of their office. The priest received a Bible. The bishop, however, did not have the Bible laid on his neck, but he was given a copy. The bishop no longer received the pastoral staff, or the shepherd's crook. In 1661 ordination at the hands of a bishop was made essential for admission to the Anglican ministry. A clear distinction was made that bishops and priests were regarded as being of different order and not simply a different degree within the ministry. Anglican ordination was severely challenged and attacked by the Roman Catholics from 1604. In 1896 Pope Leo XIII declared Anglican ordination to be invalid.

The ordination of Anglican ministers and bishops included a bidding prayer, a period of silent prayer and an ordination prayer, as well as the laying on of hands. There was a petition for the candidates that God would "endue them with all grace needful for their calling." The Anglican churches of other nations have been very conservative, and there have been few revisions in the ordination service across the centuries.

In the Church of South India the ordination service of the Church of England and the Church of Scotland have been blended into something of a union ordination rite.

### Ordination Among Methodists

John Wesley came to believe that bishops and priests differed only in degree and not in order. When the English bishops refused to provide a bishop for America in 1784, though he himself was an ordained Anglican priest, Wesley proceeded to ordain a superintendent and elders to serve there. Wesley later ordained elders for churches in Scotland and eventually those who would work in the church in England. He did this by adapting the Anglican ordination service.

The most significant change he made was to delete any reference to vesture. He also substituted the terms "elder" and "superintendent" for "priest" and "bishop" and removed all references to consecration in the ordination of his superintendents. He omitted the reference in the Anglican service adapted from John 20:23. "Whose sins thou dost forgive they are forgiven; and whose sins thou dost retain, they are retained." Candidates were given a Bible instead of just the New Testament. These services provided the basis for ordination of Methodists later in America and other countries. However, American Methodists later restored the term "bishop" instead of superintendent and used the word *consecration* which Wesley omitted. They changed the phrase, "the Lord pour upon thee the Holy Spirit," substituting for it "receive the Holy Ghost," at the laying on of hands by both bishops and elders. Earlier the candidate was examined for ordination. There was also a token election to office. There was prayer over the candidate, hymns were sung, and extemporaneous prayers offered. However, the idea of election has been played down in the United Methodist Church. In 1913 this phase was dropped altogether. In 1882 the hymn, "Come, Holy Ghost," was included in the ordination service, and this was sung immediately before the laying on of hands. A charge was delivered by the presiding officer after the observance of the Lord's Supper. He then declared that the candidate had been validly ordained.

### The Ordination of Congregationalists

Congregationalists and Baptists had a common origin in the seventeenth century among English Separatists. Ordination of Baptists and Congregationalists is very similar and is derived from the reformed tradition. Both denominations view ordination as recognition by the local congregation that a person has been called by God to the ministry and has already received the necessary gifts and graces for such. He is set apart to function as a minister within that local congregation. However, this was later expanded from simply the local church to include the wider denomination and other churches. Then the candidates were examined by a council representing this wider fellowship. At the ordination service other ministers present would preside and take part in the laying on of hands. There was an early practice of "reordaining a minister," every time he changed from one pastorate to another. This soon fell into disuse.

Among the Congregationalists from 1658 the congregation elected the minister who then was to prepare himself by a time of prayer and fasting. Hands were laid on him by the elders of the congregation. This was not considered essential but was usually the practice. Congregationalists soon abandoned the laying on of hands and substituted the giving of the right hand of fellowship instead. The ordination candidate was asked to give his testimony and tell about his call to the ministry. He would answer a series of questions, and the congregation would affirm him. After singing about the Holy Spirit, there was an ordination prayer accompanied by the laying on of hands, perhaps by representatives of the congregation and other ministers who were present. This was concluded with everyone repeating the Lord's Prayer. The presiding minister declared the candidate to be ordained and gave him a copy of the Bible. The new minister then received the right hand of fellowship from representatives of both the local and wider church. A charge was given to the minister and the congregation, and the service would end with the newly ordained minister giving his blessing.

## Baptist Ordination Practices

In an article on the Baptist heritage of ordination, Robert A. Baker wrote: "At least one statement may be made about the Baptist view of ordination without any possibility of successful contradiction: Baptists anywhere in the world have never totally agreed on the question of ordination."[4] As with other doctrinal questions among Baptists, there is a wide variety of views as to the significance of ordination.

Basically, Baptists have a nonsacramental view of ordination (as of baptism and the Lord's Supper). Some agree with Charles Haddon Spurgeon that ordination is unnecessary, "laying empty hands on empty heads." Others, including the Sandy Creek Association in North Carolina, placed great importance on the rite. Without proper ordination they felt a minister would not be a proper administrator of baptism and the Lord's Supper.

Baptists also disagree as to whether a person is ordained to a function within the church (to act as pastor) or whether ordination is a setting apart to the official ministry. Both views are held, and Baker contends that the Baptist views of ordination involve "both/and" rather than "either/or."

The two fundamental views of ordination are sacramental and evangelical. In the sacramental view the act of ordination, including the laying on of hands, is a means of divine grace. In this rite the candidate is supernaturally transformed in character—into a priest of God. And he receives a new authority—that of the clergy, with authority to forgive sins. He must have hands laid on him by a bishop who is in the line of apostolic succession from the time of Christ. Once ordained a priest he is always a priest. His ordination is absolute.

Early ordination was the setting apart of a local pastor to his ministry within a congregation. But the sacramental view of ordination was expanded to require ordination at the hands of a properly ordained bishop. At the time of the Reformation the Roman Catholic view required:

1. Ordination on the proper authority, the Church.

2. Ordination by a proper adminstrator, a bishop who was in the historical apostolic succession.

3. Ordination required a proper intention, to set a man apart to the ministry.

4. Ordination by the proper form, anointing and the laying on of hands by those in the apostolic succession.

The ordination of a bishop required the participation of at least three other qualified bishops and papal approval.

Once ordained, in the sacramental view, the priest's character was changed indelibly and forever. Ordination authorized the priest to transform the bread and wine of the Eucharist into the actual body and blood of Christ—reenacting the sacrifice of the cross. It also gave him power to bless, govern the congregation, preach the Word, administer the seven sacraments, and forgive sins.

Three major church groups hold a sacramental view of ordination: Roman Catholics, Eastern and Russian Orthodox, and the Anglican churches.

The second view of ordination is an evangelical one. It grew out of the Protestant Reformation and the teachings of men like Martin Luther and John Calvin. They denied that ordination is a sacrament which transforms the character of the one ordained and grants him the authority of the clergy. The view of the importance of historical apostolic succession was eliminated. Their emphasis was on the rediscovery of the New Testament teaching on the priesthood of all believers.

Other reformers such as the Anabaptists insisted on the ordination of only charismatic or spiritually gifted ministers.

Baptists belong to that school of thought which holds to an evangelical and nonsacramental view of ordination. We have tended to emphasize the functional more than the official nature of ordination and the ministry. For example, some churches and associations have ordained men simply to serve in a given local church. On moving to serve another congregation he would have to be "reordained."

Still others have viewed ordination as setting a person apart to the gospel ministry in a more general sense. Thus, one ordination was viewed as sufficient for a lifelong ministry in a number of churches.

Ordination may also have an even wider connotation. Persons are ordained to the ministry-at-large. They may serve as military or institutional chaplains or evangelists carrying out an itinerant ministry. In recent years some persons have been ordained to various aspects of ministry within the church such as music, education, youth, and so forth. It is the author's view that ordination is appropriate for a person who exercises a ministry within the local church or denomination. However, it would be best not to limit their ordination too narrowly. Let them be set apart to "the Gospel Ministry" though their area of specialty may be more narrowly defined within a given congregation.

Most Baptists hold that ordination sets a person aside to a ministry which is both functional and official. It is a time for "a formal dedication of the spiritual gifts of a person called of God for service and a notification to the Christian community that the person was qualified to administer the ordinances," according to Baker.

Baptists do not believe that ordination to the ministry conveys an indelible character. In fact, as a matter of church discipline, ordination may be revoked by a local church. It is even possible for a person later to be reexamined and reordained (though such an occurrence is rare).

Ordinarily a person is not ordained until being called to a specific place of service: a pastorate, church staff position, chaplaincy, and so forth. Baptist polity dictates that the local church has the authority to ordain ministers and deacons. However, ordination usually occurs within the wider context of a presbytery (made up of ordained ministers) or an ordination council (made up of ordained ministers and deacons).

Sometimes this council is designated by the district association. Still the group acts on the invitation of a local church and reports to the church its recommendation for or against the candidate's ordination.

Among most Baptists, the ordination service is conducted on the authority of the congregation at the recommendation of the council. Baptists in Britain, Canada, and the northern United States lean more toward ordination at the hands of a denominational council. Southern Baptists generally use a special council or presbytery made up of men from neighboring Baptist churches and the ordination service is within the local church.

Baptists also vary in who lays hands on the candidate. Three different practices are followed:

1. Only ordained ministers lay hands on the candidate for ordination.

2. Ordained ministers and deacons present take part, including visitors who are not members of the local congregation.

3. Increasingly, the entire congregation present is being invited to lay hands on the head of the person being ordained.

### Historical Perspective on Baptist Ordination

Let us take a closer look at Baptists' understanding of the nature of the ministry and ordination practices. Baptists have placed emphasis on the fact that every believer is to be a witness to his faith. Therefore, ordained ministers are not raised above ordinary Christians. Their ministry is not one of official status so much as one of function. They are freed from financial concerns in order to devote themselves more completely to the church's ministry.

While the ordained minister may be committed to the task of preaching, at the same time the church may have a number of gifted lay preachers. In most churches laymen also participate as worship leaders as well, even carrying out the observances of the church ordinances. A large number of Baptist pastors are bivocational, and some are not paid by their churches. The primary essentials for being ordained a minister are a divine call to proclaim the gospel and evidence of possessing the gifts of ministry.

Baptists carried the Protestant Reformation to its logical conclusion. In this sense we are the "Protestants of the Protestants" though we often like to deny that we are Protestants at all. Baptists rejected infant baptism and returned to the New Testament practice of believers baptism by immersion. Baptists rejected any form of denominational hierarchy and returned to the New Testament pattern of congregational church government. Historically, we have rejected all pressures toward creedalism, taking the New Testament as our "sole rule for faith and practice." We also rejected the state-church concept for a free church within a free state—with separation of church and state.

This same kind of radical reformation theology is found in the Baptist understanding of the ministry and ordination to the gospel ministry. The New Testament is our authority to be understood with the aid of the Holy Spirit.

Baptists believe in the necessity of a divine call to the ministry. H. Wheeler Robinson, an English Baptist, insists that "the office grew out of the gift, and not vice versa." A person is first set apart by God and then by the church. Ordination is simply the church's recognition of the person's call and gifts for ministry. Therefore, we make no great distinction between clergy and laity. The ministry of a layman, deacon, or pastor does not differ in nature, only in kind.

Baptist polity is reflected in the fact that the calling and ordination of a candidate for the ministry are in the hands of the congregation. It is not reserved to a group of bishops or elders. A church may recognize the call and gifts of one of its own members and call him out for the ministry.

## Early Baptist Practice

In the seventeenth century Baptists were anxious that ordination not be misunderstood as granting some authority to the minister. Therefore, some churches omitted ordination altogether. Others would have a service in which hands were laid on their minister. However, he was considered ordained for ministry in only that local church.

To underline the doctrine of the priesthood of all believers, some early Baptist churches laid hands on all members following their baptism. Thus, all believers were considered called to the faith, filled with the Holy Spirit, and set apart to the service of God. In modern times, Baptists extend the right hand of fellowship to newly baptized members instead of laying on of hands.

Historically, most Baptist churches have refused to set educational qualifications for the ministry. A number of early Baptist pastors were highly educated in theology. But the rank and file were not so concerned about having a trained ministry. Among Baptists on the American

48

frontier, an antieducation bias was often found. The first Baptist college founded to train ministers was in Bristol, England, in 1720. Spurgeon's College in London trained nearly 900 men for the ministry prior to the time of his death.

Roger Williams was a graduate of Cambridge University and a minister of the Church of England. He became a prime leader in the fight for religious freedom after immigrating to New England. The city of Boston was only five years old when Williams arrived. He was made an assistant in the churches there, but was too outspoken for the establishment. He was banished from the Massachusetts Bay Colony in 1635 and founded the Colony of Rhode Island in 1638 with its famous guarantee of religous liberty. This was the first civil government to do such. He established what is today the First Baptist Church of Providence in March 1639. Williams was typical of early Baptist leaders in America. Educated in England, he was endowed with a rich cultural background.

Another early Baptist leader was John Clarke. He was trained in medicine in Holland and practiced in London for a time. He was a man of outstanding abilities with education in both law and theology. He came to New England seeking freedom of religion but was disturbed by Puritan intolerance. He established a Baptist church in Newport, Rhode Island.

Another Baptist minister, John Miles, came to Massachusetts in 1662. He was the founder of Baptist churches in Wales as early as 1649. He had been pastor of the Baptist church in Swansea. He established a Baptist church at Rehobeth in 1663 and served as its pastor until his death in 1683.

Morgan Edwards was born in Wales in 1722 and trained for the Baptist ministry at the seminary in Bristol, England. He served as pastor of First Baptist Church of Philadelphia and later in Delaware from 1770 until the time of the American Revolution. Edwards realized the importance of a trained ministry and helped to arouse the Philadelphia Baptist Association to establish the Rhode Island College in 1763.

Some of the early American Baptist pastors were not trained in England but were laymen who were pressed into service and eventually ordained because they obviously had the gifts of the ministry. One of these was William Screven, a prosperous merchant, who came from England to Massachusetts and then to Kittery, Maine. He became a Baptist in 1681. He influenced a number of other people to be baptized and then was chosen as their pastor. Baptists came under persecution and were threatened with fines and penalties. Screven was summoned to court and accused of offensive speeches on the subject of baptism. He was put in jail and later fined and forbidden to hold religious services in his home or elsewhere. He was exiled to South Carolina where he purchased an estate near Charleston and preached from 1683. Baptists became increasingly concerned about a trained ministry and established academies and colleges for this purpose.

The Great Awakening had a significant influence on the Baptist ministry in America. It swelled the ranks of Baptist membership, bringing many former Congregationalists and New Lights into the Baptist churches. Between 1740 and 1776 the number of Baptist churches increased from 60 to 472. Later, revivals brought hundreds of members into the membership of Baptist congregations. The need for a trained ministry became increasingly apparent. The result was the organization of the Triennial Convention, the founding of Columbian College, Shurtleff College, and Furman University. After 1850 there emerged a settled ministry among Baptists.

[1]Henry Bettenson, *Documents of the Christian Church* (London: Oxford U. Press, 1956), p. 89.

[2]Robert G. Torbet, *The Baptist Ministry Then and Now* (Philadelphia: Judson Press, 1953), p. 9.

[3]Alan Richardson, *Theology of the New Testament* (New York: Harper & Bros., 1958), p. 332-33.

# 3.
# Toward a Theology
# of Ordination

This chapter constitutes a brief summary statement of the author's understanding of the practice and significance of ordination for Baptists.

The word *ordination* comes from the Latin *ordinationem* and the French *ordinare.* It's basic meaning is "to arrange or dispose in ranks." The term came to be used for the admission of a man to the ministry of the church or "holy orders." Behind this meaning was the concept of one's appointment to a post by divine action. Hence, he is ordained of God.

In modern practice, ordination is that service of public recognition by which the church sets apart one of its members. The person is believed to be God-called to the ministry and endowed with the gifts of the ministry.

Ordination is a symbolic and highly significant action for both the church and the candidate. However, it is in no sense a sacramental experience; some "means of grace" which conveys an indelible character to the candidate. It does not admit him into some superior clergy class. Rather, it is a recognition of his or her divine call and gifts for ministry within both the church and the world.

An examination of the biblical and historical practice of ordination proves both interesting and surprising.

The New Testament says precious little about the practice and significance of ordination. Its few references are rather ambiguous. The modern reader is tempted to read his own view back into the scant New Testament references.

The reason for little guidance on the subject is found in the nature of the early church. It was an excited and exciting fellowship. For one thing, the imminent return of Christ was expected; therefore, any organizational structures were temporary and only for the interim.

51

Further, the New Testament church was at an early stage of development. Definite organizational structure was only beginning to emerge. They didn't even need such documents as the New Testament so long as the twelve were alive and preaching.

As the church spread across the Roman Empire and became increasingly Gentile, greater structure was required and evolved. The church took a cue from the Roman gift for organization and a hierarchy developed, with the monarchical bishop at the top. The preservation of sound doctrine and the need for unity in the church led to the development of a priestly type leadership. With the passage of time ordination acquired a sacramental character, becoming highly developed beyond its New Testament roots. Indeed, the Mosaic and Aaronic priesthood of the Old Testament became the church's pattern for its ministry.

Baptists belong to the radical wing of the Protestant Reformation which sought to restore the modern church to the New Testament pattern. Thus, we rejected any concept of the priesthood except that of Christ and all believers. Along with this, we see the ordination of deacons and ministers as being more to a functional than official ministry. Ordination does not have a sacramental significance for us. Rather, it is a setting apart of a member to his or her spiritual ministry within the priesthood of all believers.

## The Priesthood of All Believers

Any consideration of the significance of ordination must be set in the broad context of the doctrine of the priesthood of believers. We believe that Jesus Christ is our great High Priest. On the cross he was both priest and sacrifice. Now he is interceding for us in the place of honor—at the Father's right hand. He came to show us the Father. In his human/divine nature and by his death and resurrection, he has brought man to God, effecting reconciliation.

Therefore, every believer is a priest before God. Each may enter the Father's presence through faith in Christ alone. Each is also responsible to share his or her faith in a personal priestly ministry. Thus, we believe in the ministry of the laity.

The deacon or minister is not admitted to some superior priestly caste by ordination. Ordination is not a sacrament, but a symbolic setting apart to a more intense or specialized ministry within the household of faith.

Those ordained are "first among equals" and are honored not for their position, but for their faithfulness as they function and exercise their gifts in ministry.

Ones view of ordination should always keep in mind the priesthood of the believer. It is a healthy corrective to the unscriptural concept of a sacramental priesthood.

## Recognition of a God-called Ministry

Baptists have historically insisted on a God-called ministry within the ministry of all believers. Thus, ordination (like baptism) is an outward recognition of an inward and spiritual reality.

The gospel minister is one who has experienced this divine inner call and has shown evidence of having gifts for ministry. The mystic call is an intuitive and inescapable sense of "ought" within the person. It may defy description, but it is an essential qualification for ordination. It is the second question to be put to a candidate after asking him to relate his conversion experience. And yet, among Baptists, the inner or secret call alone is not enough.

There also must be corporate recognition by the church. Otherwise, ordination is not appropriate or forthcoming. A church recognizes the candidate's gifts for ministry and evidence of his or her divine call. This is followed by the church extending its call to the person to serve in a place of ministry. Only after such a specific call from a church is ordination appropriate. It requires both the mystical inner call and the practical call of a congregation or Christian institution to specific a place of service.

## Ordination Is a Setting Apart for Service

Ordination has a very practical dimension. It is not so much admission to the ministry of the whole church as it is setting one apart to the function of ministry within a particular congregation or Christian institution.

William E. Hull states his view of the basis of ministry and ordination:

In brief, my view of ordination is rooted in the theology of ministry, which is profoundly Christocentric. That is, there is only one valid Christian ministry, and that is the ministry of Jesus Christ himself. Therefore, there is not ordination to many ministries, but only to His ministry. Since every Christian is called to minister in the name and spirit of Christ, ordination does not limit ministry to a few pastors and deacons, but rather focuses on those persons who have gifts to equip or enable the entire church to become ministers. In other words, ordination is an act of the church by which it identifies those with gifts of the Spirit to stir up the practice of ministry within the whole Body.

W. Morgan Patterson reflects the dual nature of ordination as both a divine and human activity:

I believe that ordination does possess considerable significance as it symbolizes in a specific act a special commitment to a form of ministry, carrying with it weighty responsibilities suggested in the New Testament. The act of ordination becomes a public recognition of something God has already done and which the people of God simply affirm in a solemn way.

Jimmy R. Allen, past president of the Southern Baptist Convention, shares his understanding of ordination:

I believe that the early church was led of the Spirit to set people aside for particular tasks and signified that by the prayers and laying on of hands. In the laying on of hands, there was a testimony of relationship. I do not see it as ritual so much as the relationship of a family designating this member or a part of it for this particular responsibility and praying for the Holy Spirit to empower him for it while signifying that oneness in the laying on of hands. It is obvious that the laying on of hands came in several ways besides the setting aside for tasks. It also was sometimes connected with the very experience of the filling of the Spirit in deeper ways in believers' lives.

I believe, therefore, that God calls people both through their gifts and the inner mystical communication of His guidance for their lives to the preaching of the gospel. This call is affirmed by the family of faith as they discern the gifts and as they rejoice in the willingness to exercise them. The specific laying on of hands probably happened more than once in a person's life and happened as they took up particular tasks. For instance, Paul and Barnabas were sent on their way on a mission journey. There was probably a specific task for them in that journey to which the church was bearing witness and giving encouragement.

There has grown up a practice of ordaining people to a state of being. We have followed the practice in conformity basically to the structures of our society and the practices of other religious groups. Therefore, the ordaining process has become somewhat altered in our practice from what the New Testament strategy actually was.

The paucity of direct instruction in the New Testament about the ordaining and laying on of hands leaves us having to fashion some of our own ideas and applications by interpretation rather than instruction. Therefore, it has been difficult for me to decide to challenge the whole stream of the way we have dealt with the ordination of ministers to the gospel. What I've chosen to do in a practical way as for my own life is that I have had a dedication service in which I have asked the church to follow the very basic pattern of an ordination while not calling it that. When I came to the task of the First Bapist Church of San Antonio pastorate, I felt profoundly moved to have such a service. In our case, the deacons of the church represented the congregation in the laying on of hands and the dedication of me to the task of the pastorate of this church.

In similar fashion, I believe that the deacons were also set aside for a particular task or assignment. There probably were other people who had different assignments who were similarly treated by the call of the congregation and the dedication to the task. Periodically in our church, we do have a service of dedication for ministers in the laity who have particular tasks. We have done this with street ministers, with Mission Service Corps volunteers, and so forth. In those times, we have called on those who felt led of the Spirit to join in a support of them to come forward and lay hands on them. Some of our most profound spiritual experiences in corporate worship have been provided by such experiences.

Among Southern Baptists, there are two schools of thought about the significance and permanence of ordination. One view might be characterized as a narrow view of ordination. The priesthood of all believers is used to level the ordained ministry. Thus, ordination is set within the context of the believer's common call to faith. Since all are called to faith and ministry, the pastor or minister is merely called to a given function within the church. His ordination then is to that specific function within a given congregation. It is not viewed as ordination to the gospel ministry in general. When a person transfers from one church or position to another, he should be "reordained." The advantage in this view is that it does not consider a person ordained for life. Thus, when he leaves the ministry, he is no longer considered an "ordained minister." It would make ordination correspond roughly to periodic installations in given places of ministry.

The second view of ordination might be called broader (but still not sacramental). It holds that a person is divinely called to the gospel ministry for life and his or her ordination is once for all. Isaiah's call becomes the pattern for the minister's call. After his vision and confrontation with the claim of God in the Temple, Isaiah asked, "How long, O Lord? And he said: 'Until the cities lie waste without inhabitant, and houses without men, and the land utterly desolate'" (6:11, RSV). The ministry is considered a call to spiritual combat which knows no discharge.

This means that ordination is a once-in-a-lifetime experience, not to be repeated. It would be revoked if the minister became a heretic or immoral, but not because he ceased to function as a minister in a particular church for a time.

Installations in subsequent churches to which the minister is called become a kind of reaffirmation of his ordination and a rededication to the gospel ministry. I share this second view of the nature of ordination. It is once-for-all—an act of obedience to the divine call and an affirmation of the church's call to minister.

## The Significance of Ordination

The practice of ordination is very simple. After the candidate has satisfied an ordination council as to his conversion, call to the ministry, and doctrinal soundness, he is set apart.

The basic ingredients in an ordination service are two: prayer and the laying on of hands. We have scriptural warrant for this simple practice.

Ordination has a number of dimensions. We do not believe in the Petrine succession of the bishops of Rome. Nor do we feel it necessary to be in some historical line of succession from the apostles. Still ordination does occur within the context of the history of our spiritual forebearers. We are debtor to all that is worthy which has gone before us. And heaven's grandstand will witness how faithfully we run. No person is ordained in a vacuum. We are part of out heritage and it is part of us.

Ordination is a public recognition of the candidate's private call to the ministry. It is also an affirmation that he or she gives evidence of having the gifts of ministry. There is a corporate dimension to ordination. It is not a private affair or something available by mail order. It involves the recognition and affirmation of the church.

Therefore, ordination has great significance for the church. God has paid her the compliment of calling one of her own into the gospel ministry. Thus, ordination is a historic moment. The church has a continuing responsibility to the persons she ordains. She should follow their ministry and spiritual pilgrimage with interest and supportiveness. The church's involvement should not end with the pronouncement of the benediction at the ordination service. Let the bond between ordaining church and candidate be a close one.

Ordination to the ministry has great significance for the candidate. This service represents his or her dual commitment—to the Lord and to the church of Jesus Christ. Ordination should occur only after the candidate has responded in obedience to the divine call. It is a sign that the person is acting according to the lordship of Christ.

Ordination is a time for spiritual self-examination and dedication on the part of the candidate as well. Let all the candidate's motives be laid bare before the Holy Spirit. He should experience both the confession of sin and the assurance of divine pardon. Ordination represents a total commitment of one's life to the will of God, yet to be revealed. It is an oath of loyalty to the King of kings, as well as the acceptance of a special ministry within the church.

A parallel could be drawn between the significance Jesus saw in his baptism and the minister's ordination. The deep significance of ordination is relived each time the minister goes through an installation service. Both represent his commitment to the will of God and to the service of the church.

In his will, John Calvin referred to himself as "servant of the Word." That is an apt title for the great reformer—and for every gospel minister. We are servants of the Word of God, both the written Word, the Bible, and the living Word, Christ. And the minister is servant of the people of God, the church. Ordination is not a solitary affair. We are ordained within the context of the family of faith and in obedience to a divine call.

# 4.
# The Practice
# of Ordination

In this chapter we will consider some practical questions in relation to Baptist ordination among some other Baptist conventions and unions.

## Who Can Be Ordained in a Baptist Church?

Theoretically, any member whom the church considers qualified for the ministry may be set apart by ordination. Baptist polity recognizes each congregation as autonomous. Therefore, there is no higher authority within this denomination which can dictate who the local church may or may not ordain.

In actual practice, sister churches do have an influence in the matter of ordination. Many churches make use of the district association's ordination council in examining candidates. Even when this is not done, most churches will call a council including ministers from neighboring congregations. Thus, there is almost always a broader representation in ordination than the local church.

As noted in the section on ordination among other Baptist bodies, the practice varies. Some require strict adherence to educational standards. However, Southern Baptists are so insistent on local autonomy that it would be very difficult for them to set and enforce standards for ordination. American Baptists (principally in the Northern United States) have established educational standards for ordination. They require a college degree and a three-year course in a theological seminary, or the equivalent. However, in actual practice this is at times difficult to enforce due to autonomy of local congregations.

Ordination standards are difficult to enforce among Baptists since each church is self-governing. Yet the force of the tradition of including representatives from other congregations does contribute to continuity in ordination practices and a broader base than just one church.

## Who Should Be Ordained?

While theoretically any member of a Baptist church could be ordained, who should be? While the practice of each local congregation may vary, the candidate's qualifications should include:

1. A person who has had a genuine conversion experience. A cardinal doctrine of Baptist ecclesiology is a regenerate church membership. We do not hold a parish view which requires that everyone living in a given district is a member of the local church. Rather, we insist that the membership of the church be made up only of born-again believers who have made a public profession of faith and followed Christ in baptism by immersion. Since this is the case, the first requirement of a minister or candidate for ordination is that he give evidence of having had a spiritual rebirth. If the minister is to lead the church and lead the lost to faith in Christ, he or she must know the Lord firsthand. This should be the first question put to a candidate by the ordination council: "Relate your conversion experience and your spiritual pilgrimage to date."

2. The second qualification for ordination is a sense of divine call to the ministry. Baptists insist on this. Only the call of God should get a person into the ministry—for nothing less will keep him there. Such a sense of call may be dramatic or gradual, but it should not be absent. The prophets of the Old Testament and inspired preachers of the New spoke their message with a sense of divine compulsion.

The ministry is God's business, and his ministers should be divinely called to it. There is no standard way in which the call can be described. It varies from person to person, as does our conversion or call to faith. While each call is unique, a calling is essential if one is to be a minister.

The one basic point of difference in the functioning of an ordination council examining a minister or a deacon is found just here. The minister is asked to relate his or her call to the ministry. This is often termed one's "call to preach." While deacons have a personal lay ministry, such a question is ordinarily not asked in their ordination council.

3. The minister being examined for ordination should be doctrinally sound. While some fine points of interpretation may not be identical with those of the council members, there should be agreement on basic biblical doctrine. If the candidate is confused, untrained, or not settled in his

doctrinal views, his ordination might well be postponed. Just because a church has called for a person's ordination and just because a council has been convened does not mean that a candidate must automatically be ordained. Indeed, it may be the responsible recommendation of the ordination council that the candidate not be ordained, or that ordination be postponed until he is better prepared.

It is important that candidates be well-grounded in the faith. They should not be a novice or new convert (for their own good and the church's). Indeed, we have the biblical admonition, "Lay hands hastily on no man" (1 Tim. 5:22, ASV). This would certainly apply to a candidate who held heretical views or one who had a weak foundation in the faith.

4. A person to be ordained must be of high moral character—above reproach both within the church and in the community. It would be a mistake to ordain a man of questionable character. One who is not honest or is immoral would bring reproach on the ministry and the church. While this qualification is self-evident, it has not always been adequately taken into account.

5. The candidate should have the confidence of his fellow church members. Ideally, they should know him well and have had opportunity to judge his character and gifts for the ministry. While it is not always possible for the congregation to know the candidate well, still it is desirable. Ordination is a commendation of a person by one church to other churches. Therefore, the ordaining church should satisfy itself as to the qualifications of the candidate.

6. Ideally, the candidate should first be licensed to preach or minister. This gives the church an opportunity to observe the life and gifts of the candidate prior to his ordination. There is usually no set time between licensing and ordination. It may be a fairly brief or a long time. Some men have been licensed but, not being called to serve a church, have never been ordained. They simply continue to serve as a "licensed minister." In customary practice licensing precedes ordination and is preparatory to it.

Sometimes a person is called to a church or other place of ministry and is examined and ordained without being licensed. In Baptist polity this creates no problem. Normally, a young person will be licensed to preach when they announce their call to the ministry. This may occur as they enter college or the seminary. However, in most instances, they would not be ordained until called to a church.

7. Preferably someone who has been called to a position of ministry

61

should be ordained, and not before such a call is extended. Sometimes churches ordain a person who is entering seminary. Or they may ordain him on the completion of his theological training. Candidly, this is sometimes done in order to help an inexperienced minister "get a church."

Such a practice is questionable. Ideally, the candidate should first be called to a place of service and then ordained. Failure to wait on a call has resulted in many persons being ordained ministers; embarrassed at having never served a church. They may exercise significant lay ministries, but this does not require ordination. The churches should act more responsibly with reference to whom they ordain.

Graduation from seminary does not necessitate ordination for Baptists. It may be expected or automatic in some other denominations, but they have a bishop or system of placement which Baptists lack. It is best to delay ordination until one is called to a specific place of ministry. This fulfills the threefold call: the call to believe, the inner or mystic call to the ministry from the Lord, and the corporate call of a congregation or Christian institution to a place of ministry.

Persons should be ordained who intend to minister within the denomination of the church which calls them. We are ordained as ministers of Baptist churches. While we recognize and appreciate our fellow ministers in other denominations, each ordains its own.

## When Should a Minister Be Ordained?

A church should not be in too big a hurry to ordain anyone. In writing to Timothy, the apostle Paul pleaded that care be taken in recognizing a person as a minister of the gospel (5:22). Observation would bear out the wisdom of that caution, in the modern church. It should not be lightly administered lest its worth and importance be devalued. Let the church be careful about the hasty and indiscriminate ordination of anyone.

Sometimes a church will hastily ordain as a deacon or minister someone who has recently had a glorious or dramatic conversion experience. We do not do such a person a favor by ordaining him. Premature setting apart may contribute to the minister's or deacon's undue pride—most unbecoming. More often than not, the newly ordained person becomes disillusioned. His white-hot enthusiasm may be suddenly cooled by the lethargy of older Christians. He may become disappointed by a bad experience in the ministry to the point of bitterness.

It is wise to follow the biblical instruction to let the candidate first prove himself. Some spiritual maturity is desirable. An opportunity to exercise his gifts of ministry within the church and community will be reassuring to both the church and the candidate. Enthusiasm is a desirable quality, but it is not the only one required in ministry. Perseverance in adversity is also important, along with theological training. The old adage still applies: "a call to preach is a call to prepare" to the limits of one's ability.

Don't ordain anyone too soon.

## What About Educational Requirements for Ordination?

In many mainline denominations ordination occurs only after one has received a four-year college degree and a basic three-year course in a theological seminary (currently the Master of Divinity degree). Some Baptist bodies exert pressure in this direction, setting educational minimums for ordination. However, this is difficult to enforce since each local Baptist church is autonomous. These Baptist denominations insist on a minister's compliance with certain standards for national recognition by the denomination.

Southern Baptists have recognized the importance of theological education for their ministers. This has been a concern from the beginning of our denomination. Early Baptist colleges in the south were vitally concerned for a trained ministry. This was a factor in the establishment of such institutions as the University of Richmond, Wake Forest University, Furman University, Mercer University, Samford University, Mississippi College, Baylor University, Georgetown College, and so forth. Concern for theological education was paramount in the thinking of those who organized the Southern Baptist Convention in 1845. This is clearly evidenced by their establishment of the Southern Baptist Theological Seminary in Greenville, South Carolina, in 1859.

In 1978 Southern Baptists enrolled 11,000 students in their six theological seminaries and contributed $20,912,000 toward their training. In addition, the denomination reported another 11,000 students in Baptist colleges and universities who were headed toward church-related vocations. Over a ten-year period seminary enrollments showed a 79 percent increase (1968-1977). Twenty-three percent of the denomination's Cooperative Program gifts go to theological education.

Thus, we see there is a strong emphasis on preparation for ministry among Southern Baptists. However, while the subject has been debated

63

periodically, the denomination has refrained from setting educational standards for ordination. This is considered to be the function of the local church, not the denomination.

In actual practice there has been pressure toward a better educated ministry. Thoccurred not so much at the hands of ordination councils but by pulpit committees or pastor selection committees and church personnel committees. They normally insist on educationally qualified persons to fill ministerial posts within the churches. Thus, there has been a practical pressure encouraging educational preparation. While the denomination has not set standards for ordination, the churches are increasingly requiring such qualifications in the persons they call.

However, a theological degree does not constitute a "union card." The churches consider many other attributes as well. These include such things as a sense of divine call, preaching ability, personality, and experience in the church life and ministry.

Some 30,000 Southern Baptist pastors serve our 35,000 churches. The average church has a membership of 373. As the educational level rises nationally, it also rises among the ministers. The churches are placing greater importance on theological education. Still in actual practice a person may be ordained a Southern Baptist minister by a local congregation with little or no formal theological education.

## How Is One Licensed to the Gospel Ministry?

When a young man gives evidence of the gifts of the ministry, he should be encouraged to exercise those gifts. Licensing of ministers should be a preliminary stage in their preparation and should take the place of premature ordination. A candidate for licensing should be examined as to his experience and purpose in Christian work. If he possesses the proper qualifications, he should be counseled as to his preparation and recommended to his church for licensing. There may be a service of recognition connected with the granting of the license. The candidate is customarily invited to preach at the service. Often it is his first sermon. Among American Baptists the license is issued for a limited time, subject to renewal. In this way, it is possible to keep in close touch with young men who are looking forward to the ministry.

A Certificate of License is provided by the church, bearing the signature of the moderator and clerk of the church. It is presented to the candidate at the time of the service of recognition.

Among Southern Baptists the common practice is to license a person when they acknowledge their call to the ministry. It may occur as he or she enters preparation for the ministry by going to college or seminary. The license is a recommendation to sister churches that the minister has given evidence of a divine call and exemplifies the gifts of the ministry. The license may read: "John Brown is hereby licensed to preach the gospel, as he may have opportunity . . . ."

Generally, a "license to preach" leads to ordination. However, the license does not ordinarily entitle a person to perform weddings. This may vary from one state to another according to law. In most cases the licensed minister would not lead in the observance of the Lord's Supper or baptize. However, he could be authorized to do so by the local church (as could any member, since the authority rests with the congregation).

While some churches may limit the time in which the license is valid, most make it indefinite. A license may be revoked by the church on such grounds as heresy, immorality, or disloyalty to the denomination.

Ordination occurs after a church has voted to call for the ordination of a candidate; after he or she has been examined by an ordination council or presbytery; after the council has recommended ordination; and after the local church has voted to proceed with the ordination of the candidate.

## Steps in the Process of Ordination

Customarily, the church which has called a person to a place of service "calls for" his ordination to the gospel ministry. That church may call a council or presbytery to examine the candidate. Or it may communicate with the candidate's home church, or the church in which he currently holds membership. That church would then call the council to examine the candidate.

The ordaining church votes to authorize its pastor or deacon chairman (if the church is without a pastor) to call an ordination council or presbytery. (An ordination council is made up of ordained Baptist deacons and ministers. A presbytery is made up of ordained ministers only.) Normally, the council is made up of ministers and deacons from the ordaining church and from neighboring Baptist congregations.

The candidate may be consulted as to whom he would like invited to serve on the council. It might be meaningful to the candidate to have a former pastor, a college or seminary professor, or a relative take part. However, the responsibility for determining the makeup of the council usually rests with the pastor of the ordaining church. Care should be taken to make the council representative.

65

Some district Baptist Associations have a standing committee which constitutes an ordination council. Usually the church is free to use or not use the association's council. However, if it is not used, care should be given to have churches from the association represented in the makeup of the group.

The ordaining church or her pastor sets the time for the candidate's examination by the council (in consultation with the candidate, of course). Care should be taken not to schedule the council meeting just prior to the planned service of ordination. This could avoid embarrassment. Councils may vote to postpone recommending the candidates ordination, or they may vote to recommend that he not be ordained. This would prove awkward if the ordination service had already been announced. Don't be presumptuous. As a general rule, it would be wise to conduct the examination of the candidate by the council two weeks or more prior to the anticipated ordination service.

Some churches conduct the examination before the entire congregation, immediately prior to the ordination service. While there are values in such a public examination, there are also opportunities for embarrassment and disaster. The candidate feels enough pressure in facing the council privately. It could be even more awkward if the examination were conducted publicly.

The church clerk or pastor of the ordaining church sends letters of invitation to sister churches or neighboring pastors to participate in the council. The letter may follow a simple format such as this:

*Dear _____:*

*The River Oaks Baptist Church of Dupont, North Carolina, has called Brother Ralph E. Webb to be their pastor. Mr. Webb is a member of the First Baptist Church of Greensboro. The River Oaks Church has requested that he be examined for ordination to the gospel ministry.*

*I would like to invite you to serve as a member of the presbytery to examine him for ordination. We will meet in the pastor's study at the church, 1000 West Friendly Avenue, at 2:00 PM, Tuesday, May 15. You may respond by returning the enclosed card.*

*I look forward to serving with you on this significant occasion.*

*Sincerely,*
*Philip R. Jones, Pastor*

The Card:

_____*I will be happy to participate as a member of the presbytery to examine Ralph E. Webb for ordination to the gospel ministry, at First Baptist Church of Greensboro, Tuesday, May 15 at 2:00 PM.*
_____*I will be unable to serve.*

_____

*Signed*

The ordination council or presbytery meets at the announced hour. The first order of business after introductions is for the council to organize itself. The host pastor usually presides. A moderator is elected. He then presides for the election of other officers. These include a clerk who keeps minutes of the council's proceeding. A copy of which will be read or given in brief at the ordination service. A copy should be made a part of the minutes of the ordaining church. Another copy should be presented to the candidate on the day of his ordination.

The council elects an examiner who leads in the questioning. He asks the candidate:

1. To relate his conversion experience and the high points of his Christian life up to the present.

2. To relate his call to the ministry.

3. To express his understanding of key biblical doctrines. These may include such subjects as:

- the nature of God;
- the person and work of Christ;
- the person and work of the Holy Spirit;
- the candidate's understanding of the Scriptures as the Word of God;
- how one becomes a Christian;
- the nature of the church, its ordinances, government and membership;
- the officers of a New Testament Baptist church and their role;
- the doctrine of Christian stewardship;
- the candidate's understanding of and loyalty to the denomination;
- the candidate's commitment to missions and missions support;
- the candidate's understanding of the role of a minister in the church and community;
- the candidate's plans for continuing theological education.

While the examiner leads in the questioning, other members of the council are free to ask questions at any point. When the questioning is complete, it is appropriate to ask each council member if he has further questions.

Once the questioning is completed the candidate is dismissed. The council deliberates its decision, allowing each member to share his impression of the candidate's worthiness. After ample discussion, the moderator asks for a motion expressing the will of the council. The motion is seconded and discussed. A vote is taken.

The candidate is asked to reenter the room. The moderator informs him of the council's decision and recommendation to the church.

If the council's decision is positive, the members of the council are invited to sign the ordination certificate. It will be presented to the candidate at the service of ordination. Of course, the council may recommend that the church proceed with the candidate's ordination; not ordain him; or delay his ordination until certain conditions have been met, such as the completion of his theological education.

The clerk of the ordination council notifies the church of the council's recommendation. If it is positive, the church proceeds to set a date for the ordination service.

The church clerk or pastor of the ordaining church publicizes the ordination service by:

1. Writing a letter to neighboring congregations to invite their members to attend and their ministers and deacons to take part in the laying on of hands. A simple format:

*To the members of Walnut Street Baptist Church,*

*We are happy to announce a service of ordination to the Christian ministry for Brother Ralph E. Webb. The River Oaks Baptist Church of Dupont, North Carolina, has called him to be their pastor and requested his ordination. A presbytery of nine Baptist ministers examined the candidate on May 15 and unanimously recommended that he be ordained. The First Baptist Church has voted to proceed with a service.*

*We wish to invite the members of your church to join us in the service of ordination at 7:00 PM Sunday evening, June 15 at First Baptist Church. The ordained ministers and deacons of your congregation are invited to participate in the laying on of hands.*

A reception will be held honoring the candidate and his family following the service of ordination. We hope you can join us for this significant occasion.

Sincerely,
Philip R. Jones, Pastor

2. Letters should also be sent to relatives and friends of the candidate, inviting them to be present for the service. The candidate will furnish a mailing list of these.

Dear _____:

We are sure you rejoice with us in the call of Ralph E. Webb to be pastor of the River Oaks Baptist Church in Dupont, North Carolina.

We want to invite you to be present at 7:00 PM on Sunday evening, June 15 at the First Baptist Church of Greensboro, 1000 West Friendly Avenue. A service of ordination will be held for Brother Webb with a reception to follow. We do hope you can be present.

Sincerely,
Philip R. Jones, Pastor

3. The church clerk or pastor of the ordaining church should also send a news release to local newspapers and the state Baptist paper, announcing the ordination:

Dr. Philip R. Jones, Pastor
First Baptist Church
1000 West Friendly Avenue
Greensboro, North Carolina 27403
Phone: (919) 274-3286

### For Immediate Release

GREENSBORO, N. C.—Ralph E. Webb, 23, the son of Mr. and Mrs. Emerson Webb of this city, will be ordained to the Baptist ministry on Sunday afternoon, June 15.

The service, which begins at 7:00 PM, will be held in the First Baptist Church here, where Webb grew up and was baptized at the age of 13.

After graduating from the Grimsley High School as an honor student, Webb completed his undergraduate work at Campbell University. He graduated in June from *The Southern Baptist Theological Seminary in Louisville, Kentucky. He was teaching assistant to Professor Dale Moody.*

*He also served as assistant pastor of the Broadway Baptist Church in Louisville. Mr. Webb has been called as pastor of the River Oaks Baptist Church, Dupont, North Carolina. It was the River Oaks Church which requested his ordination.*

*The candiate's brother, Wayne E. Webb of Columbia, South Carolina, who is also a Baptist minister, will deliver the main address. The candidate's father, who has been a Baptist deacon for 37 years, will lead the prayer of ordination.*

*A public reception will follow the service in the church fellowship hall, according to Dr. Philip R. Jones, pastor of Greensboro's First Baptist Church.*

The pastor of the ordaining church plans the order of service, in consultation with the candidate. Persons are enlisted to bring the ordination sermon or "charge to the candidate" and to lead the ordination prayer. Someone is designated to present the ordination Bible to the candidate. (It is provided by the ordaining church and should be appropriately inscribed with the candidate's name, the occasion, and the date. It may be signed by the pastor and other participants in the service.) Persons may also be chosen for the invocation, benediction, and to lead in the reading of a litany of ordination. Special music should be planned.

The pastor will also order an ordination certificate, have it filled in and framed, for presentation to the candidate at the close of the service.

The ordination should ideally be at a stated worship time on Sunday morning or evening. However, it may be held as a special service on another day or on Sunday afternoon. The pastor will see that a reception is planned to follow the service. It is especially nice to have representatives from the candidate's new pastorate present for the service and reception. A series of follow-up news releases may be sent to the local papers and Baptist state paper. They should include a glossy photograph of the candidate, and may include a picture of the principal participants in the service. The pastor should arrange to have a photographer at the ordination service and reception. An album of photographs may later be presented to the newly ordained minister as a keepsake. News releases may be sent to local newspapers and to the newspapers in the city where

70

the ordinand will serve as pastor. If appropriate, they may be sent to more than one state Baptist paper.

## Check List for the Pastor of the Ordaining Church

_____ 1. Confer with the candidate concerning his desires for ordination and plans for the council and service.

_____ 2. Present the request of the church which has called the candidate, asking for his ordination, to the ordaining church.

_____ 3. The church authorizes the pastor to call an ordination council or presbytery. He sets a time for it to be convened.

_____ 4. Issue invitations to the ordination council, in consultation with the candidate.

_____ 5. Preside over the council until a moderator is elected. Be sure each person present is introduced to the group.

_____ 6. See that the council's recommendation is reported to the church. Ask the church to vote to proceed with a service of ordination, setting the time and place.

_____ 7. Notify the candidate's church of plans for his ordination, inviting them or their representatives to attend.

_____ 8. Invite neighboring churches to attend the service of ordination.

_____ 9. See that appropriate news releases are prepared and sent out.

_____10. Plan the order of service in consultation with the candidate, and invite service participants.

_____11. Be sure an ordination certificate and Bible are secured and properly inscribed. The candidate may be asked to select the type Bible and translation he prefers.

_____12. Preside over the ordination service. Arrange a reception and photographer.

_____13. See that follow-up news releases are prepared and sent out.

### Some Examination Questions

The examiner elected by the ordination council may ask such questions as:

• "Please relate your conversion experience and the beginning of your life in Christ."

• "What persons were instrumental in your accepting Christ as your Savior?"

- "Share the highlights of your discipleship to date."
- "Tell us about your call to the ministry."
- "As we come to an examination of your doctrinal understanding, tell us what you believe about:

The nature and eternal purpose of God;

The dual nature of Jesus as both human and divine;

The significance of Jesus' teachings and ministry;

The meaning and value of his death and resurrection;

The person and work of God, the Holy Spirit;

The nature, ordinances, and offices of the church;

How one becomes a Christian;

The polity or government of the church;

The pastor's role in the church, community, and denomination;

Your understanding of Christian stewardship;

Your plans for further theological education as a pastor;

How would you function in a church with a multiple ministry?

How do you feel about the importance of missions?"

The above list is not intended to be exhaustive, only suggestive. Obviously, the candidate's responses will suggest further and more specific questions. Additional questions will relate to personal and ministerial ethics. The council may also raise questions about the candidate's personal evaluation of himself and his future plans. The moderator should see to it that the questioning moves along and does not bog down in theological hairsplitting or controversy.

The candidate's pastor may have a preparatory meeting with him. He should be told broadly what type of questions to expect, such as his conversion, call, and doctrinal understanding. The candidate should be reassured of the council's sympathetic attitude toward him.

At the reception, the candidate may be informally congratulated at the front of the church following the service. If a more formal reception is given, the receiving line could include the candidate, his family members, and persons who participated in the ordination service. A love offering or gift may be presented to the candidate at the reception, but this is not an expected practice.

## A Pastor's Preparation of the Candidate

The following letter was written to a prospective ordination candidate in preparation for his meeting with the council:

Mr. Ralph W. Turner, Jr.
4901 Latimer Rd.
Raleigh, N. C. 27609

Dear Wertie:

Thank you for responding so quickly to my letter. I have met with the deacons and we feel the date for the examination should be Friday, April 20th, 1979, at 8 PM. Assuming that all goes well on that evening, we will schedule the Ordination Service for Sunday afternoon, April 29, at 3 PM.

In preparation for the examining council, would you please prepare and mail to me a biographical sketch so that it can be duplicated for distribution at the Friday evening meeting? In addition, I am listing in this letter a series of questions which you should be prepared to answer during the examining council. You will want to remember that these are the questions which will be put to you in one manner or another by the chairman of the council and, in addition, you should be prepared for other questions which could come from any member present. Please remember that the purpose of the examination is not to validate your call, which is divine, but rather to attempt to arrive at a human understanding of whether or not you are prepared to respond in a meaningful manner to the call. Here are the questions:

1. Explain your concept of God. Include in your explanation details relating to God as Father, as Son, and as Holy Spirit.
2. Share with the examining council your Christology. This should embrace such areas as the Virgin Birth, Atonement, Death, Resurrection, and so on.
3. State your understanding of the doctrine of man, his creation, fall, regeneration, justification, and sanctification.
4. What is your concept of the church? Deal with such terms as the Body of Christ and a local group of baptized believers.
5. Be familiar with the relationship of the local church to the association, the state convention, and the Southern Baptist Convention. In addition have some general knowledge as to how these various groups function.

Now, Wertie, I have not tried to include every area which will probably come up for consideration; however, I do think I have shared with you the major areas. Primarily, I think I can say you need to be very certain as to what you believe, and you need to be able to give an account of the reasons as to why you hold the beliefs you have embraced.

Unless I hear from you further, I will assume the dates and times we have shared in this letter are agreeable and we will proceed with our planning along these lines.

Please give my regards to the family.

Sincerely,
William L. Tomlinson, Pastor
First Baptist Church
Newport News, Virginia

## Baptist Ordination Practices
## In Other Conventions and Unions

There are many common beliefs and practices among the Baptists of the world. However, it is interesting to note ordination practices among several different Baptist conventions and unions.

### *American Baptist Churches, U.S.A.*

This is a major convention of Baptists found predominately in the northern and western United States. They were once called the Northern Baptist Convention. They number 1,593,000 members. William R. McNutt has written about ordination from their perspective. He contends that ordination is by the local church. It ordains one who is within its membership; preferably one who is to be its minister. The ceremony of ordination is a public "setting-apart" of the candidate to the ministry of Christ and his gospel. The ordination service is planned by the ordaining church in consultation with the candidate.

Theoretically, the local church has complete authority in the matter of ordination, but in practice few churches assume to act independently. Ordinarily, a given church is in fellowship with other Baptist churches, through the Association ... and consequently it seeks their counsel in the important matter under consideration. ... A man once ordained becomes either an asset or a liability *to all the churches*. ... Neighboring churches are requested to send representatives, including their ministers, to form an examining council which shall determine the fitness of the candidate for the high calling of a minister in Christ.

With growing frequency such a council is permanently organized and it is representative of all the Baptist churches within the given Association. Such a permanent council has such officers and committees as it may find helpful. It is self-determined and usually meets annually at the time of the Associational gathering for the election of officers and the transaction of other business. Special meetings are called whenever any church desires the counsel of the other churches concerning any matter related to ordination.

The candidate is requested to appear before this council for examination. The inquiry aims to ascertain the genuineness of his Christian experience, the reasonableness of his call to the ministry, and the acceptability of his views of Christian doctrine. The relative importance given to these items depends, of course, upon the composite mind of the council. The ideal is that sufficient types of minds may be represented so as to secure a fair and genuine examination at all three points.

The examination concluded, a vote determines whether or not to advise the inquiring church to proceed with the ordination.

Caution is the mood that becomes a church when it contemplates ordination. None would question its right to ordain a minister for itself. Here the local church is regarded as wholly competent, but that it is competent to ordain *for others* is not granted, and just here rises the urgent need for caution.

Ordination is held by Baptists to do nothing magical or sacramental to the minister; it is only a formal way of setting him apart for a particular work among the churches. Ordination empowers him to administer the ordinances of baptism and the Lord's Supper, and in general, to perform the services of a good minister. Beyond these matters, ordination is held not to vest any power in him not resident in any other church member.

"Conduct unbecoming a minister" is considered sufficient grounds for the church that holds his membership—upon the advice of a regularly constituted council of churches—to revoke his credentials.

Here we note that while the local autonomy of the churches is preserved, emphasis is also placed on the corporate nature of ordination. While ordination practices vary from one area to another among Southern Baptists, American Baptists appear to make more uniform use of the Associational ordination council.

## British Baptist Ordination Practices

Ernest A. Payne has written about the ordination practices of Baptists in the British Union of Great Britain and Ireland. "We think of the function of the ministry in terms of leadership rather than of government and discipline." This functional view of ministry rejects the idea that ordination is essential to the existence of a true Christian church. This is obviously in reaction to Anglican views of apostolic succession as essential to an authentic ministry. However, British Baptists do believe a ministry is essential for the church's greatest effectiveness.

British Baptists feel that the laying on of hands at ordination services is a recognition of the broader aspects of Christian fellowship. It is a reflection of the interrelatedness of the local congregations. J. S. Whale wrote: "Ordination to the ministry is a spiritual act of the whole church, and though entirely within the competence of the local church, it invariably takes place in the presence of and with the assistance of representatives of other gathered churches."[1]

Payne further contends, "We hold firmly the priesthood of all believers, and therefore have no separated order of priests. The ministry for us is a gift of the Spirit to the Church and is an office involving both the inward call of God and commission of the Church. We can discover no ground for believing that such commission can be given only through an episcopate, and we hold that the individual Church is competent to confer it. For us there is no more exalted office than a ministry charged with preaching the Word of God and with the care of souls. Those called to devote their whole lives to such tasks are held in special honour. Yet any full description of the ministerial functions exercised among us must also take account of other believers, who at the call of the church, may preside at the observance of the Lord's Supper or fulfill any other duties which the Church assigns to them."[2]

From the beginning British Baptists have had an exalted concept of the office of the Christian minister and have taken care to call men to serve as pastors. The minister's authority to exercise his office comes from the call of God in his personal experience. This call is tested and approved by the church of which he is a member and by representatives of the larger churches. He receives intellectual and spiritual training and then is invited to exercise his gift in a particular sphere. His authority is from Christ through the believing community. It is not derived from a chain of bishops held to be linearly descended from the apostles. A man who is called is not only the minister of a local church but is also a minister of the whole church of Jesus Christ.

Among British Baptists, ordination takes place when a man has satisfactorily completed his college training and has been called to the pastorate of a local church, appointed to a chaplaincy service, or accepted for service abroad by the Committee of the Baptist Missionary Society. The ordination service is presided over by either the principal of his college, a general superintendent, or a senior minister and is shared in by other ministers and lay representatives of the church. There is no prescribed and set form of service. It invariably includes either a personal statement of faith or answers to a series of questions regarding the faith. From the seventeenth century on, ordination took place with the laying on of hands. In the nineteenth century this custom fell into disuse, but it is now again increasingly practiced by British Baptists.

Dr. Dakin, President of Bristol Baptist College, gave a helpful statement of the British Baptist view of the ministry and ordination.

All the members of a Baptist church are regarded as of equal standing before God whose grace in its fullness is available for all while at the same time there is recognition of diversity of gifts. There are different functions, for example, administration, presiding at church meetings, conducting worship, teaching, preaching, presiding at the ordinances, conducting wedding and funeral services, and the cure of souls.

Now there is nothing in Baptist theory to prohibit any member of the church doing of these things provided that he has the gifts and is properly appointed by the church to do them. As a matter of fact, many a layman has exercised a cure of souls as effectively as any minister. There is, indeed, no difference in the Baptist view between the layman and the minister so far as the gift of grace is concerned. All spiritual endowment is open to all, and it is maintained that the inspiration of the divine Spirit is as necessary for fulfilling for the office of deacon or Sunday School teacher as for presiding over the church's minister . . . .

It follows that Baptists have no "order" of ministry in the sense that there is in the church a class of men made distinctive by some special endowment of divine grace regarded as being conferred by an ordination ceremony, or the laying on of hands, or in any other way.

The setting aside is important. It means that he gives his whole time to the work, and it is usually assumed that he will devote his whole life to it.

In the setting aside for the ministry, it is held that both God and the church play a part. There is first the divine call in the soul and then the recognition and ratification of such call in some way by a church.

The divine call is felt to be absolutely necessary. A man does not appoint himself; nor does the church acting alone single out a man for the task, though sometimes, as we should expect, a divine call comes to a man through the discernment and encouragement of the church—witness, for example, the call of John Bunyan.

A man's call comes to him in his inner life in the dealings of God with his soul. It is bound in some way to be related to the Gospel, though there is no reason why it should concern itself in every instance with preaching. The cure of souls may be as intense in a man's desire as the preaching of the Word; he may feel himself called to be a pastor even more than a prophet, but to be this as it may, he has a conviction borne in upon him that God is calling him to give his whole time to the work of the Kingdom. Normally, this comes about because he has already been exercising his particular gift in the church to which he belongs, and it is the success he has met with in so doing that enables him to hear the divine call. Having heard the call, and desiring to respond to it, he continues to exercise his gift, and begins to think of preparation for the ministry. Actually, some success in the work is required at this stage before he receives any encouragement to proceed further.

The part played by the church has always been insisted on in the Baptist body. The man's call must in some way be tested before it is accepted. In the early days the testing was in a man's home church. Usually he preached two or three times before the members, and was then by vote of the church either rejected, or deferred for a time or accepted. If accepted, he was sent out to preach in neighboring churches wherever he found opportunity. Then if a church invited him to the pastorate, he was permitted to settle down to the regular ministry.

Today a candidate must have the recommendation of his home church before proceeding to college. Then he must be approved by the college committee, a body of representative Baptists. During his college days he continues to exercise his gifts. Then when his college course is complete to the satisfaction of the committee, he is ready to receive an invitation by a church to become its minister. Such invitation is regarded as a further confirmation of the call. When he is actually in charge of the church, he is then entitled to look upon himself as a Baptist minister. The invitation, of course, is not given without previous inquiry into his character and service, and the recognition of the Baptist Union of Great Britain and Ireland is of value. A man is a Baptist minister when:

1. He knows himself called of God to the work;
2. When that call has been recognized in some way by a Baptist church after careful inquiry; and
3. When he is actually exercising a fulltime ministry in a Baptist church.

What happens when a man gives up his church? There is no sense in which a man can claim to be a Baptist minister when he is not the head of a Baptist church. He may, of course, still have his name on the Baptist Union list of those who are regarded as qualified to exercise the office, but that is a different thing. There is actually no minister without ministering.

Neither is it possible on sound Baptist principles to speak of being a minister of *the* Baptist church. Among Baptists, ministering is defined primarily in terms of the local community and not in terms of a central authority or of an ideal whole.

Baptists believe that every true Baptist church is an expression and part of the Church of God. Therefore, every Baptist minister of a Baptist church, is, ipso facto, a minister of the Church of God only, in Baptist theory. He is not first a minister of the Church of God in some general way and then minister of the church at Corinth. Rather, the situation is exactly the reverse. First, a minister of the local church, and then by reason of that, a minister of the Church of God.

The nature of the ordination service, which is held when a minister begins his first church, is naturally determined by the conception of ministry as set out above. It is usually called an ordination service, though obviously the word is used in a sense different from that which it carries in the communities that believe in "orders." The Baptist view is that the true and only adequate ordination is by the Spirit of God. The church needs to recognize this, to acknowledge it, and gladly acquiesce in it . . . . Hence, there is usually a clear statement by the candidate of God's dealing with him leading to his call, and also a statement by a representative of the church accepting him in the name of the church as its minister. Beyond these statements, addresses may be given dealing with the work of ministry and the obligations on either side. These, however, are only exhortations, and ought not be allowed to overshadow the two statements of minister and church.

Needless to say, the ordination prayer is held to be of great importance. All come together with deliberate intent to seek the blessing of God from the beginning, and everything is regarded as being by God's grace and by his power. Thus, God rules his church.[3]

## Ordination Practices by Baptists in Scotland

Andrew MacRae indicates that among Scottish Baptists when a man is ordained there are representatives from his home church, from the church which has called him to be pastor, from the Baptist Assciation, and from the Ministerial Recognition Committee of the Baptist Union. This committee is made up of five persons. A man is given a two-day examination in order to be qualified and recognized as a minister by the Baptist Union of Scotland. He is questioned on his call to the gospel ministry and on his academic and theological preparation to be a gospel minister. He is also questioned as to his understanding of church life and Baptist polity. He is questioned by a pastor and a psychiatrist concerning his personality. He must submit an extensive biographical statement. Only after these two days of intensive examination is he recommended by the committee for recognition by the Baptist Union for ordination to the gospel ministry.

## Ordination Among Canadian Baptists

Ordination among the Canadian Baptist churches is highly centralized. Their practice is similar to that of Scottish Baptists. There are close ties between the two groups.

When a local Baptist church wishes to ordain a candidate, it calls on the Association Ordination Council. Or in the case of churches in the western part of the nation, examination for ordination is conducted by the ordination council of the Baptist Union of Western Canada. At the annual meeting, the council takes its place in the choir loft of a church, while delegates to the denominational meeting fill the pews.

The ordinand is thoroughly and publicly examined as to his call to the ministry, his doctrinal understanding, his educational preparation for the ministry, and his denominational loyalty. The examinations may consume a full day as a number of ordinands appear before the council.

The council's recommendation for ordination is reported to the local church where the service is then conducted. The recommendation of the associational or denominational ordination council is required if a minister is to be recognized. Without such approval, a minister's name would not be listed in the denomination's annual; he would not be recognized for participation in the denomination's annuity program. Neither would he be recognized for the chaplaincy or other recognition required by the state.

## Nigerian Baptist Ordination Practices

*Some Principles of Ordination.* (1) Ordination is on the authority of the local church. In the Nigerian Baptist Convention, the churches have chosen a Ministerial Board to help in ordination. The authority rests, however, in the local churches. (2) The Ministerial Board represents the churches as an examining and guiding council. It is not authoritative, but advisory. (3) Churches should be careful not to seek the ordination of a pastor too early. He will serve churches throughout the Convention and is therefore a blessing or hindrance to the entire Convention. Ordination indicates "blanket approval" of a minister's qualifications and (pastoral) experience, before all denominations and non-Christians. (4) Neither should churches be too hesitant to recommend men who have proved themselves before the Convention. The quality of the men who are already ordained may largely determine the willingness of churches to ordain others. (5) The church must seek ordination for the pastor, and not the pastor for himself.

*Qualifications for Ordination.* In addition to the personal qualifications given previously, these other qualifications seem wise before ordination. (1) *Character.* A pastor must have proved himself to be of commendable Christian life and character. It does the Christian cause great harm to ordain a man of unproven or unworthy life. (2) *Divine call* to the ministry. Men do enter the ministry with unworthy motives. One must give assurance by deed and service that he has been called of God. (3) *Educational preparation.* A call to the ministry is a call for preparation. Educational preparation becomes more necessary as the general educational level of the country rises. Men from both the Certificate and Degree Departments of our Seminary have been ordained. (4) *Experience on the field.* One is not ready for ordination until he has been tested and tried on the field of service. He must have proved himself able to withstand the temptations, trials, hardships, and responsibilities of a pastor. Some may prove this in a short time, while others may never rise above doubts and questions. (5) *Doctrinal belief.* Ordained pastors are the recognized representatives of our churches in the Convention. We must be sure that they are doctrinally sound and able to give an account of the faith which they hold.

## The Baptist Union of Sweden

Erik Ruden, General Secretary of the Union, gave an overview of their ordination practices:

The first Swedish Baptist minister was baptized in Hamburg in 1847. When he came back to Sweden he clearly saw that he could not take it upon himself to preach the Gospel or to administer the sacraments of Baptism and the Lord's Supper. Since the Swedish Baptists were considered a part of the German Baptist Union, ordination took place in Hamburg at a request from the Swedish Baptist congregation. The importance of ordination was very highly regarded by the German Baptists. Nobody was allowed to preach if he had not been ordained. Very few were ordained and the appointment was held to be for life. At the ordination service prayers were offered by ordained persons, accompanied by laying on of hands.

When the Swedish Baptists organized an association of their own they followed the pattern of the German Baptists. This is to say that the qualifications of a candidate were examined by older experienced pastors, the act took place in a local church, and this church was looked upon as representing "the wider Church." Missionaries to foreign fields became ordained at a special service at the annual conference of the Baptist Union. This practice is still followed and is applied not only to ministerial candidates but also to nurses and teachers. There is no fundamental objection against such a service being held in a local church.

About forty years ago a special act of prayer for graduating students began to take place at the termination service of the Bethel Seminary. This act is now a part of the Home Mission Service at the Convention. How is the act of prayer performed and what is the meaning of it? The Principal of the Bethel Seminary introduces the graduating students whereupon the Mission Director of the Baptist Union puts the following questions to the candidates: (1) Are you sure that God has called you to be servants of his Word? (2) Are you willing to commit your lives to the holy service as ministers of the Baptist Union of Sweden? (3) Are you willing to keep under the seal of silence what has been confided to you as confession of sin in your capacity of pastors?

Prayers are offered, accompanied by laying on of hands by the Mission Director, the Professors of the Bethel Seminary, the President of the Baptist Union and some others, not necessarily all of them ordained persons.

The young pastors attach great importance to the act of prayer because it gives them recognition as ministers and representatives of the Baptist Union. I think that this opinion is an expression of the reaction against calling ministers who have too incomplete education for the great task of serving in the ministry of the Church. Still it is not easy to find a good formula for the relation between the act of prayer at the annual conference and the ordination in the local church. It has been said that the former is the occasion when the Seminary commits the graduating students to the Baptist Union for their service in the Union. The latter is an authorization to the exercise of a pastor's ministry in the local church.

The ministral ordination takes place at a special ordination service in the church which has called a person to the ministry, and this church asks for his ordination. There are few pastors who ask for re-ordination when moving to another church. The act of ordination is usually conducted by the Superintendent. Sometimes the Principal of the Bethel Seminary or an older Baptist minister serves as ordainer. The fellowship with the wider Church is observed in that other churches in the area send representatives and Baptist pastors often take part in the act of ordination. The candidate for ordination has to answer four questions concerning (1) his stewardship as a servant of Jesus Christ, (2) his task as a preacher of the Gospel, (3) his task as a pastor and teacher, and (4) his own devotional life. In connection with prayer, laying on of hands is practiced. The persons laying on the hands are the ordainer and the pastors who take part in the service.

As a fundamental qualification, the candidate must know that he has been called by God to serve in the ministry of the Word. He must have been chosen by God for this task. Women are equal in every respect, and this year two women are to be graduated for the ministry.

What is the meaning of ordination? On the part of the candidate it is an act of consecration and commitment to the work of the ministry. The ordination gives the new pastor the authority that is founded not in a service ordained by men but by Jesus Christ himself. On the part of the church it is an act wherein the church authorizes and sets apart a disciple of Jesus Christ for the work to which he through the Holy Spirit has been called and endowed. In the ordination of a person the church testifies its spiritual responsibility for the pastor. The ordination is also an act wherein God manifests his election of his servant and gives him power for the work. This is also expressed by the laying on of hands. Among the Baptists of Sweden not only pastors but also deacons are ordained as a special act, usually in connection with a communion service. Prayers are offered accompanied by laying on of hands. During an earlier period of the history of the Swedish Baptists the deaconship was for life, but nowadays the churches more and more elect their deacons for a period of 5-6 years.[4]

## Australian Baptists Ordination Practices

Australian Baptists Ordination Practices are described by J. G. Leigh Wedge.

Ordination in Australia is a mark of education and professional training as well as of recognition of the call of God. A man is not ordained until he has received professional training in a theological college, which is the name we give to our seminaries.

The various State Unions recognize three classes of men doing the work of the ministry. There is the ordained minister in full standing, the pastor who has had no seminary training but has been called to serve a local church as its minister, and there is the student pastor who is in training. The churches preserve their autonomy by calling whom they will, but they co-operate with the State Unions by calling their minister either the Reverend Mr. X or Pastor Y.

The ordination service is generally held during the State Union Assembly Meetings when the Union officers and representative ministers lay their hands upon the heads of the kneeling ordinands. An ordination sermon or charge is given by one of the ministers.

The practice of ordaining men in their home church after they have been trained and accepted for ordination by the Union is beginning to operate. At these local ordination services the officers of the Union are helped by representative ministers of the local District Association.

The ordination practice of Australian Baptists rests upon their view of the church. We believe that the church of Jesus Christ is the whole body of believers for whom Christ died and which one day will be assembled before his throne as his bride. We also believe that a church is a local body of believers, designated in the New Testament as the church at a particular place. We do not believe that the Union or a denomination is a church or exercises any authority over a local church. The local church can call whom it will be be its minister. But in ordination we set apart a man to the ministry of Jesus Christ and not to a local church. This is why ordination is regarded as the responsiblility and action of all the churches met in conference. This is also the reason why the local Baptist churches in Australia do not ordain men to the ministry. They do not ordain deacons or deaconess either.

Australian Baptists regard the laying on of hands as symbolic of the fact that the churches are laying the man aside to the full-time work of the ministry of Jesus Christ. The ordination does not put the man in a holy class apart, nor does it mean that his service is rendered more acceptable to God. Rather is it the recognition that the man has been called by God and accepted and trained by the churches to devote all his time to the ministry of the Word and the promotion of the cause of Jesus Christ the Lord.[5]

[1]J. S. Whale, *The Ministry and the Sacraments (1937), 214.*

[2]*The Fellowship of Believers* (London: Carey Kingsgate Press, 1952), p. 158.

[3]A. Dakin, *The Baptist to You of the Church and Ministry* (London: The Baptist Union Publication Dept.; 1944), pp. 41-48.

[4]*Review and Expositor,* Vol. 55, Issue 3, 1958.

[5]*Review and Expositor,* Vol. 55, Issue 3, 1958.

# 5.
# Ordination
# Services and Sermons

This chapter contains materials which could prove useful as resources for planning ordination services and sermons. It includes suggestions for use in the ordination of both ministers and deacons.

## An Ordination Prayer

*Father, we thank you for your servant, John Davis, his faith in you, and his answering your call. We are grateful that you have obviously given him the gifts of ministry. And that recognizing his qualifications, this congregation has called him to be their pastor.*

*We pray for him now, as he kneels before you. Grant him a deep sense of your Presence, the enduement of God, the Holy Spirit, and devotion to the gospel of Christ.*

*May John minister not in his own wisdom, but in yours. Make him faithful to his calling, that he may be greatly used of you.*

*Bless his family and help them to be supportive of him and the task to which you have called him.*

*Father, we pray that John's ministry may further the gospel in the earth, bringing many to faith and maturity. May the Lord Christ be exalted as he serves as preacher/pastor in this congregation and beyond.*

*Now, in prayer we ask that you would set John apart for service in the gospel ministry, in the name of God the Father, Son, and Holy Spirit. Amen.*

## Ordination Sermon Seed

The following consists of some thoughts on the pastor's role as a "dangerous opportunity." Mahan Siler is Director of the School of Pastoral Care in Winston-Salem North Carolina.

### Pastor's Role

A pastor: fully human, yet a special representative of the divine; sinful yet proclaimer of the sacred in our midst; fellow believer who both needs a pastor and is a pastor. On and on the list of "both-ands" could go.

So, it goes—the pastor can be both the man behind the pulpit and the man behind the "eight-ball."

I've come to a fresh awareness of the dangerous opportunity of serving as pastor. For the pastor I see two pitfalls. On one hand, he/she may become so open and receptive to the ambiguities and sufferings of people that he/she loses perspective, giving way to fatigue and discouragements. Is there a profession that requires such an on-call exposure to the joys and sorrows of the human experience? Emotionally, it's a roller-coaster vocation.

Or on the other hand, I detect the opposite temptation of withdrawing from such intensive involvement, becoming a professional juggler of religious ideas and symbols. We may become a mere mouthpiece of the gospel, evading the realities of daily living behind the benevolent authority of the role. We can easily confuse our "set apart for ministry" with being special, deserving special privileges. The result of this path is loneliness and lack of authenticity. To avoid such pitfalls a pastor must have a strong inner life, a deep sense of being centered in a God-given worth not so attached to performance.

As I see it, the pastor is special and set apart but not because he or she is more righteous and less caught up in the common conditions of humanity. The pastor is a simple man or woman who is special because he or she has tasted a vision of the love of God and is enabled by the congregation to dedicate his or her total professional life and skills to living out that vision with a congregation.

### Paraphrase on Psalm 1

Pastor: The man who chooses to live a significant life is not going to take his cues from the religiously indifferent.

**People: Nor will he conform to the crowd.**

Pastor: Nor mouth his prejudices.

**People: Nor dote on the failures of others.**

Pastor: His ultimate concern is the will of God.

**People: He makes his daily decisions in respect to such.**

Pastor: He can be compared to a sturdy tree planted in rich and moist soil.

Pastor: His life is productive and effective.

**People: This is not true concerning the ungodly.**

Pastor: They are like sand in a desert storm.

**People: Or leaves in an autumn wind.**

Pastor: They cannot stand against the judgments of the eternal God.

**People: And they are most uncomfortable amongst those who demonstrate genuine faith in the God of righteousness.**

Pastor: The children of God walk in the course that God has ordained.[1]

---

[1]From *Good Lord, Where Are You?* by Leslie F. Brandt.

## A Litany of Our Calling
### (Based on Isaiah 61)

To what has God called us?
    TO BRING GOOD TIDINGS TO THE AFFLICTED.
To what has God called us?
    TO BIND UP THE BROKEN HEARTED.
To what has God called us?
    TO PROCLAIM LIBERTY TO THE CAPTIVES.
To what has God called us?
    TO THE OPENING OF THE PRISON,
    TO RELEASE THOSE WHO ARE BOUND.
To what has God called us?
    TO PROCLAIM THE YEAR OF THE LORD FOREVER.
To what has God called us?
    TO COMFORT ALL WHO MOURN.
    TO ALL THIS, AND MUCH MORE GOD HAS CALLED US.

The church is the called community of the faithful.

You are a chosen race, a royal priesthood, a holy nation, God's own people, that you may declare the wonderful deeds of him who called you out of darkness with his marvelous light. Once you were no people but now you are God's people; once you had not received mercy but now you have received mercy (1 Pet. 2:9-10, RSV).

The church is you. The church is me. The church is persons—persons called by God and claimed by God.

Who me? Yes, you! We are not our own. We belong to Christ—we are God's own.

Called—as Noah, to build an ark when the sun was shining.

Called—as Abraham, to go he knew not where and he knew not how.

Called—as Moses, to lead when he stuttered and stammered and could not speak.

Called—as Jonah, to preach to a people he despised.

Called—as Isaiah, who felt the numinous presence of God in the Holy Temple.

Duke University Chapel<br>
The Reverend Robert T. Young<br>
Minister to the University

## Ordination Service
## for
## DAVID HUGHES
## November 6, 1977
## 3:00 PM

**PRELUDE**   "He Who Will Suffer God to Guide Him"   Bach
**SOLO CALL TO WORSHIP**   "Thou Art Worthy"
Donna Forrester
**SPOKEN CALL TO WORSHIP (In Unison)**
We are a chosen race, a royal priesthood, a holy nation, God's own people, that we may declare the wonderful deeds of him who called us out of darkness into his marvelous light.
**HYMN OF ADORATION**   "A Mighty Fortress Is Our God"
**INVOCATION AND LORD'S PRAYER**   Dr. Alton McEachern
**DOXOLOGY**
**PASTORAL GREETING**   Dr. Alton McEachern
**HYMN OF DEDICATION**   "Have Thine Own Way, Lord"
**REPORT OF ORDINATION COUNCIL**   Albert S. Lineberry,
Clerk of the Council
**SOLO**   "St. Francis Prayer"
Geneva Metzger
**SERMON**   "The High Calling"   Rev. S. C. Ray
**CHARGE TO THE CANDIDATE**   Dr. Charles Talbert
**LITANY OF DEDICATION**   Mike Ford
(Jer. 1:4-9; Isa. 6:8;61:1-2)

Leader:   Thus says the Lord, "Before I formed you in the womb I knew you, and before you were born I consecrated you; I have appointed you a prophet to the nations."

David:   "Alas, Lord God! Behold I do not know how to speak, because I am a youth."

Leader:   But the Lord said, "Do not say 'I am a youth' because everywhere I send you, you shall go, and all that I command you, you shall speak. Behold, I have put my words in your mouth."

David:   "Here am I, Lord, send me."

Congregation: "The Spirit of the Lord is upon you because the Lord has annointed you to bring good news to the afflicted;

89

He has sent you to bind up the broken-hearted, to proclaim liberty to the captives, and freedom to the prisoners; to proclaim the favorable year of the Lord."

**PRAYER OF DEDICATION**               Mike Ford
**LAYING ON OF HANDS**
**PRESENTATION OF BIBLE AND CERTIFICATE OF
    ORDINATION**       Franklin Paris, Chairman of Deacons
**HYMN OF PRAISE**                "He Lives"
**BENEDICTION**                 David Hughes
**POSTLUDE**     "Praise to the Lord, the Almighty"     Gesangbuch

Members of the congregation and friends are invited to
attend a reception in the church parlor.

<br>

### The Ordination
### of
### S. PERRY HOLLEMAN
### to the Gospel Ministry
### October 7, 1979, 3:00 PM

<br>

**MOMENTS OF MEDITATION**          Organist—Pianist
**HYMN**        "To God Be the Glory"      Congregation
**PRAYER**               Rev. James McKenzie
**READING OF THE MINUTES OF THE PRESBYTERY
   AND THE CHARGE TO CHURCH**      Rev. Yates Brooks
**CHARGE TO CANDIDATE**         Rev. J. D. Harrod
**HYMN**       "Lead On, O King Eternal"     Congregation
**SERMON** "I Magnify Mine Office"    Rev. Woodrow W. Robbins
**ORDINATION PRAYER**       Rev. William L. Holleman
**LAYING ON OF HANDS**
**PRESENTATION OF BIBLE**         Mr. John Gordon
**BENEDICTION**              Mr. C. H. Laws

• • •

Everyone is invited to a reception honoring
Reverend and Mrs. S. Perry Holleman
in the Fellowship Hall immediately following Benediction.

# Service of Installation
## for
## Dr. Alton Howard McEachern
### as Pastor of
## First Baptist Church
## Greensboro, North Carolina

January 27, 1974                                              3:30 PM

**PRELUDE**—Choral Prelude                                        Willan
**INTROIT**—"All Creatures of Our God and King"    *Lasst Uns Erfreuen*
**\*PROCESSIONAL HYMN** "The Church's One Foundation"    Aurelia
**\*CALL TO WORSHIP AND INVOCATION**              Rev. Del Suggs
                                    Assistant Pastor, First Baptist Church
**GREETING**                                          Mr. Seth Macon
                                    Chairman of Deacons, First Baptist Church
**WELCOME TO THE McEACHERN FAMILY**
From the Community                              Honorable Jim Melvin
                                          Mayor, City of Greensboro
From Churches of the Community          Rev. John D. Schofield
                            President, Greensboro Ministers Fellowship;
                                   Pastor, Palm Street Christian Church
From North Carolina Baptists                    Dr. Perry Crouch
                                    Executive Secretary-Treasurer,
                          Baptist State Convention of North Carolina
**ANTHEM**                    "Gloria in Excelsis"              Mozart
**THE CHURCH IN COVENANT**
Epistle—Ephesians 4:1-7, 11-13              Mr. Scott Lineberry
                                    Representing Youth, First Baptist Church
Charge to the Church                    Mrs. Arthur Shackelford
                              Director, Womans' Missionary Union,
                                            First Baptist Church
\*(Please stand and join in the congregational responses)
By our calling of this man of God to be our Pastor, we do now enter into a
solemn covenant with our Lord and with our pastor that we will faithfully
perform the tasks expected of us as members of God's family and of this
church. We will remember at all times the things which we have
covenanted to perform with our Lord and with our pastor.

91

**With thanksgiving to God for his mercy and goodness, we accept the responsibilities of our covenant.**

We promise to be good hearers and to receive the Word of truth which he preaches. We promise to encourage him in his work and to help him in his endeavor to help us, giving the prayerful thought and planning so necessary on our part.

**With the love of God in our hearts and a will to worship him and to learn of him, we accept the responsibilities of our covenant.**

We carry responsibility with him for the spiritual upbuilding of the church. We are his fellow workers. We are laborers together with him. We will pray for him and with him. We promise to make it our particular duty so to provide for him in material things that he may be free to give his time to the church and its wide ministry without distraction or unnecessary anxiety.

**With the love of this church and the love of the fellowship of all Christians we accept the responsibilities of our covenant.**

We promise, further, to do everything within our power to advance the kingdom of God in the hearts and lives of people in this city and throughout the world. This is a high obligation. It requires that we be good stewards of the time, personality, and material resources which we have received from God and that we exemplify the love of Christ toward all persons whom our influence touches.

**With a desire to honor our Lord and to advance the cause of Christ in the world, we accept the responsibilities of our covenant.**

Remember always that we are one body in Christ, and every one members of another. There is one body, and one Spirit, one Lord, one faith, one baptism, and God and Father of all who is above all, and through all, and in us all. May the blessing of God be upon us. And now unto him who is able to do exceeding abundantly above all that we ask or think according to the power that worketh in us; unto him be glory in the church by Christ Jesus, throughout all ages, world without end. Amen.

**\*HYMN**          "O God, Our Help in Ages Past"          St. Anne

**THE PASTOR IN COVENANT**

Epistle—2 Timothy 2:1-15

Rev. W. A. Duncan
Superintendent of Missions,
Piedmont Baptist Association

Charge to the Pastor                          Dr. William E. Hull
                                    Provost and Dean, School of Theology,
                                The Southern Baptist Theological Seminary
(Following the charge these questions will be asked by Dr. Hull and answered by the Pastor.)

Do you believe that you are truly called by God to this ministry in his church?

**I do so believe.**

Are zeal for the glory of God, love for our Lord Jesus Christ, and a desire to share his love and grace with all persons, so far as you know your own heart, your chief motives for entering into this ministry?

**So far as I know my own heart, they are.**

Will you be diligent in the reading and study of Holy Scripture and in such other studies as will help you to apply its truth clearly to the lives of those committed to your care?

**I will, the Lord being my helper.**

Following the example of that great Shepherd, will you minister to his people in all circumstances, identifying yourself with them in their joys and sorrows, giving special care to those who are ill, bereaved, or otherwise oppressed?

**I will, the Lord being my helper.**

Will you help your people to be good stewards of the manifold gifts of God, that every member may be equipped for the work of ministering and that the whole congregation may be built up in love?

**I will, the Lord being my helper.**

Will you endeavor to lead a prayerful and disciplined life, remembering your responsibilities as a Christian husband and father, as well as the obligations you here assume as pastor to the flock of Christ you have been called to serve?

**I will so endeavor, with God's good help.**

"You then, my son, be strong in the grace that is in Christ Jesus, and what you have heard from me before many witnesses entrust to faithful men [and women] who will be able to teach others also" (2 Tim. 2:1-2, RSV).

**PRAYER OF DEDICATION**                     Dr. Vance Havner
**HYMN**          "A Mighty Fortress Is Our God"      *Ein' Feste Burg*
**BENEDICTION**                              Rev. Troy Robbins
                        Superintendent, Masonic and Eastern Star Home

**POSTLUDE**—Fanfare Postlude: "All Glory, Laud, and Honor"
Based on "St. Theodulph"

The Sanctuary Choir, First Baptist Church

Mr. Douglas P. Peoples, Minister of Music

Mrs. Douglas Peoples, Organist

Mr. Ronald Patterson, Chief Usher

Following this service, you are cordially invited to attend a reception in the First Floor Auditorium honoring Dr. and Mrs. McEachern.

# Ordination Sermons

## GOD'S HERALD

by Alton H. McEachern
1 Timothy 1:3-7; 1 Peter 5:1-4 (Phillips)

"Now may I who am myself an elder say a word to you my fellow-elders? I speak as one who actually saw Christ suffer, and as one who will share with you the glories that are to be unfolded to us. I urge you then to see that your 'flock of God' is properly fed and cared for. Accept the responsibility of looking after them willingly and not because you feel you can't get out of it, doing your work not for what you can make, but because you are really concerned for their well-being. You should aim not at being 'Little tin gods' but as examples of Christian living in the eyes of the flock committed to your charge. And then, when the chief shepherd reveals himself, you will receive that crown of glory which cannot fade" (1 Pet. 5:1-4, Phillips).

### Introduction

S. C. Ray, this is a significant hour for you. It is the hour of your ordination to the gospel ministry. The laying on of hands does not set you above the fellow Christians conveying some special grace or privilege, but it does fix an awesome responsibility upon you. It sets you apart to a special ministry as a man of God. Once Dr. Wayne E. Oates was visiting in a hospital when a patient asked him, "Be ye the man of God?" It is a probing question to put to any minister. The answer for you must be positive.

Phillips Brooks gave us a classic definition of preaching, calling it "truth through personality." This is your task and calling. You are set apart to be a shepherd of God's people and a herald of the matchless gospel.

### The Measure of the Man of God

As a minister you have at least three callings. First, you have been called to become a Christian. You must experience the call to Christian faith as surely as Jesus called his disciples from their tasks as fishermen in Galilee, saying, "Follow me." You are one who knows Christ firsthand. Without this basic call to faith, you have no business in the ministry.

Secondly, there is the inner call or the secret call. In the inner sanctum of your own heart and spirit you have been confronted by the claims of Christ. You have felt a persuasion, indeed a compulsion, to answer God's call to the Christian ministry. His hand is upon you, and he is trusting you forth into his ministry. This deep sense of divine calling is the only thing that ought to get a man into the ministry. Because nothing else will keep him there, when the going is rough.

Thirdly, you've experienced the corporate call of the people of God. The church has recognized that you have the gifts of ministry and has called you to a place of service as one of its ministers. In this way, the body of Christ has verified your inner call to ministry.

In addition to being called, you are to be a committed man. Your first commitment and chief loyalty belongs to the Lord Jesus Christ. George W. Truett once asked, "Success, what is success? To do His will, that is success!" It's this personal commitment to the Lord which will give you success in ministry—as he measures it.

Your ordination also constitutes a call to be committed to God's people; to love them and to serve them. One of the old Scottish divines is reported to have said that no man should enter the ministry who has not that quality which kindles at the sight of men. Commitment to the people of God will result in this kindling quality. The Lord said to his prophet Isaiah: "Comfort ye, comfort ye my people, saith your God" (40:1).

Leonard Small said that there will come times in a man's ministry when he will stand outside a door knocking with the secret hope that no one will answer. This may be because the minister knows that on the other side of that door is an awesome sin or a fearful suffering or a deep sorrow. He wishes the door would not open because he dreads confronting the persons on the other side. Small admonishes us to remember that Christ is on the other side of that door. Our task as ministers is to go in and make his presence known. Your commitment is to Christ, but it is also to his sheep.

## Consider the Magnitude of Your Mission

It is far bigger than you are, and there are times when it will leave you absolutely frightened.

You will be confronted with the seriousness of sin and human failure. You will encounter every human emotion: guilt, frustration, despair, joy, sorrow; both the tragic and the trivial. You will wrestle with sin in your own life, discovering the forgiveness of God. And you will wrestle with sin in the lives of others, confronting them with the call of Christ to righteousness, and sharing with them the assurance of divine pardon, following their repentance. You will share with persons in times of great joy: weddings, the birth of a child, a high honor and achievement. And you will walk with them in the valley of the shadow of death. You will soon learn that joy and sorrow often live on different sides of the same street. It is no small task to which you are called.

The magnitude of the mission will practically force you to become a man of prayer. You will have to rely on God and on prayer which lays hold on God's might. Most of the failures in the ministry are not due to a lack of study or pastoral visitation or good church administration. Most often we fail due to a lack of consistent prayer. You will be called upon to rely on the grace of God time and time again. This will necessitate your being open to the leadership of the Holy Spirit, allowing Christ to carry out his ministry through you.

W. O. Carver called the church the "continuing incarnation." The Christian ministry is not an ego trip for some prima donna. The Scripture reminds us that we have nothing which we have not received. As you see the evidence of the working of the grace of God in human lives, as you observe authentic spiritual growth and maturity in the lives of some that you have led to Christ, you will be thrown back on a basic humility. The magnitude of the task and the finitude of the preacher will be constantly before you. Alexander Whyte said: "Only once did God choose a sinless preacher." You are not likely to be the second one.

If you are really honest before the Lord, you will have to recognize that all you accomplish in winning souls to Christ, in helping Christians to grow, and in leading God's church, is really his doing through you. It is not so much your accomplishment as God's. All of life, indeed life itself, is sheer gift. Let the reality of this truth lead you to deep gratitude and committed service.

## You Are Called by God to Preach Christ

Let me challenge you to make your message and ministry Christocentric. You are called to declare the Word of God. That alone is your base of operations. As you declare and apply his Word, then you will have an enduring ministry which will last long after your voice is still. Preach Christ.

D. M. Baillie has reminded us that we stand between a memory and a hope, looking back to the incarnation and forward to the consummation. We have the high privilege of participating in God's eternal plan of the ages by sharing the gospel message.

As a minister, you will often be lonely, but never alone. You are surrounded by a cloud of witnesses. Many have gone before you: men like Peter and Paul; Augustine and Chrysostom; John Bunyan and John Calvin; George Truett and James Stewart; as well as tens of thousands of others whose names we will never know. You're in a high and holy company of men who have been called to a task the angels could envy.

You are called to be God's middleman, standing between the eternal and ordinary folk. Ian McPherson relates a story which illustrates the middleman position.

King George V of England was to deliver his first radio message to the people of America. More than a million people were waiting to hear the king's voice. Suddenly, in the radio studio in New York City a cable snapped in two. Harold Vivian, a technician, saw what had happened. The king was about to speak, and there was not time to make a repair. The technician took hold of the ends of the wires. The voltage shook his body, but the king's message got through. You are to be the channel through whom God's message gets through to the needy hearts of men. You are called and set apart to be the man of God, a man for others.

# OUR MINISTRY

## Alton H. McEachern

The questions of religious authority and the nature of ministry loom large in the history of the Christian church. In the first century, missionary apostle Paul wrote: "We have this ministry by the grace of God, therefore do not lose heart" (2 Cor. 4:1, Writer's Translation).

The church of Rome bases the authority of its ministry on Simon Peter's successor, the Pope who is called "Pontifex Maximus," or chief priest. He is considered to be infallible, not as a man, but when he speaks "ex cathedra," officially on matters of doctrine and morals.

The Church of England bases the authority of its ministry on apostolic succession through the bishops of the church.[1] The authority to be a minister is conveyed, they believe, in ordination by a bishop who was ordained in a line of succession which stretches back to the first apostles of Jesus. It is an attractive argument but one which is hard to prove historically.

Baptists belong to that school of Reformation thought which places great emphasis on the priesthood of every believer. Thus, we believe that every Christian is meant to be a minister, on mission for God. Each member of the body of Christ whether laity or clergy has a personal ministry. We stress the importance of a God-called ministry to exercise leadership within the church, but insist that every church member has a personal ministry as well.

Christ's ministry is the pattern for all Christian ministry.[2] Notice the balance in the ministry of Jesus. He spent time in solitude and prayer, and time in service: teaching, preaching, and healing. The pattern of his ministry included both withdrawal and involvement. Elton Trueblood has written helpfully of the polarization within denominations between pietists and activists, those who stress evangelism and others who opt for social ministries. One group sings, "There is a place of quiet rest, near to the heart of God," while the other militantly sings, "Rise Up, O Men of God!" Jesus' ministry reflected a much more healthy balance.

Jesus gave first priority to people. Boris Pasternak has said that in the kingdom of God there are only persons. Jesus was concerned with the whole person, body, mind, and spirit. Still he placed persons above institutions, even such cherished institutions as sabbath regulations.

In Mark 5 we have the story of Jesus healing the demoniac at the expense of a swine herd. It is startling that at the conclusion of this episode the citizens of that area came to Jesus and asked him to leave their region! Better pork than a sane citizen. Many times we, too, are tempted to value property above persons. Jesus never made that mistake. He loved all kinds of people. He spent time with people. He exercised his ministry among people.

Our mission, too, is with people. That's not easy. They are often hard to love. It is possible to "love all mankind" while despising people. Our priorities can be tested by applying three simple questions:

1. *How do you spend your time?* What claims your best energies, your highest interest? I once read that Phillips Brooks was late to a speaking engagement because he took time to see a little girl's kittens. Yet when he spoke he moved the hearts of his hearers. What interests demand your time? In the ministry of Jesus it was always people.

2. *How do you spend your money?* Everyone has limited financial resources, no matter how much they may have. What causes, hobbies, or persons claim first priority on your money? This is a basic stewardship question. Remember that Jesus said: "A man's life does not consist in the abundance of the things he possesses"; and "Where a man's treasure is, there is his heart, also" (Luke 12:15; Matt. 6:21, Author's Translation).

3. *What sort of things do you allow to interrupt you?* Obviously, many interruptions are inescapable. But what sort of avoidable interruptions do you allow to break into your schedule? This is a test of priorities.

If every Christian is a minister and our pattern of ministry is that of Jesus, what need have we for ordained ministers? There is a long history of resentment toward an established ministry in the church. After all it was a group of uptight religious leaders who had Jesus put to death. It was the "princes of the church" who conducted the inquisition, seeking to force conformity to the faith with imprisonment, violence, and executions. The Reformation was largely a revolt against the abuses of the priesthood and its acquired power. Early Quakers went so far as to reject any formal ministry within the church.

Yet we believe in a God-called ministry. Every Christian is called to faith and is to find his or her personal area of ministry. Some believers, however, are gifted and called to specialized ministries. This involves an inner or intuitive call and the external call of the church to a place of ministry. These specialized ministers are to serve as equippers of others for their ministry. This dual role is clearly spelled out in Ephesians 4:11-12:

"These were his gifts (to the church) that some should be apostles (missionaries or ones sent), some prophets (or inspired preachers), some evangelists, some pastors and teachers to equip God's people for work in his service, to the building up of the body of Christ" (Author's Translation).

In this equipping ministry the pastor and staff are in the role of a "player-coach." Note the apostle Peter's clear admonition to these ministers: "Now may I who am myself an elder say a word to you my fellow elders? I speak as one who actually saw Christ suffer, and as one who will share with you the glories that are to be unfolded to us. I urge you then to see that your "flock of God" is properly fed and cared for. Accept the responsibility of looking after them willingly and not because you feel you can't get out of it, doing your work not for what you can make, but because you are really concerned for their well-being. You should aim not at being 'little tin gods' but as examples of Christian living in the eyes of the flock committed to your charge. And then when the chief shepherd reveals himself, you will receive that crown of glory which cannot fade" (1 Pet. 5:1-4, Phillips).

The equipping ministers are to enable the laity to find and function in their own personal ministries. The first mission of the church is to worship God. The word *liturgy* actually means "the work of the people." In our worship we offer ourselves, our praise, and our gifts to God. This is our first ministry: to ascribe supreme worth to God.

Christian service and witness are the second ministry of Christians. We are the people of God on mission. Emil Brunner has said that the church exists by mission as fire exists by burning. Ministry and mission, evangelism and witness are not electives. They are required. And we cannot simply do them vicariously, by paying someone else to go in our place. Ministry is incarnational. Indeed W. O. Carver maintained that the church is "the continuation of the incarnation."[3] As we go we are to minister and witness. We will share both "our daily bread" and the "Bread of life." Find God's ministry for you, whether it is great or small.

The priesthood of all believers is a precious doctrine. It means that we have access to God for ourselves, without the necessity of going through any mediator other than Jesus. It also means that like Jesus, we are to be a "man for others"—a priest to others, bringing them to the Father. In Latin the word for priest is *pontifex* which literally means "a bridge builder."

Our ministry is to worship God, and to be a bridge over troubled waters to others. The priesthood of believers means both access to God and accountability for others. This is our ministry.

Whose woods these are I think I know.
His house is in the village, though;
He will not see me stopping here
To watch his woods fill up with snow.

My little horse must think it queer
To stop without a farmhouse near
Between the woods and frozen lake
The darkest evening of the year.

He gives his harness bells a shake
To ask if there is some mistake.
The only other sound's the sweep
Of easy wind and downy flake.

The woods are lovely, dark, and deep,
But I have promises to keep,
And miles to go before I sleep,
And miles to go before I sleep.[4]

[1]K. E. Kird, ed., *The Apostolic Ministry: Essays on the History and the Doctrine of Episcopacy* (London: Hodder and Stoughton, 1946).

[2]Leonard Griffith, *We Have This Ministry* (Waco: Word 1973), pp. 32-33.

[3]Duke K. McCall, *What Is the Church?* (Nashville: Broadman Press, 1958), p. 7.

[4]From *The Poetry of Robert Frost* edited by Edward Connery Lathem, Copyright 1923, © 1969 by Holt, Rinehart and Winston. © 1951 by Robert Frost, reprinted by permission of Holt, Rinehart and Winston, Publishers.

# CALLED TO SERVE

by Alton H. McEachern

Exodus 3:1-6

Moses was one of history's great men by any measure. Shakespeare wrote, "Some are born great, some achieve greatness, and some have greatness thrust upon them." Moses belongs to the latter group. He reluctantly became a leader of men, but he became a powerful one.

Reared in the royal palace in Egypt, he had an Egyptian name and was adopted by the daughter of Pharaoh Rameses I. He got into trouble defending the Jews and had to flee to the desert. There he met and married the daughter of Jethro, the priest of Midian. His occupation became shepherd to Jethro's flocks. Moses had time to think; time to recall the oppression of his people in Egyptian slavery. He must have asked himself a thousand times, "What can one man do?"

One day Moses led his flock to the far west side of the Sinai desert. He came to Horeb, the mountain of God. There he experienced the awesome call of God to a tough task: to become the liberator of the Jewish people.

## The Shepherd (v. 1)

Moses was busy about an ordinary task when God called him. How are we to recognize the great moments when they come? They look so ordinary. Moses' life story had been a reversal up to that time. He had gone from riches to rags.

The desert life was one of great solitude with plenty of time to think. Muhammed said, "He will never be a prophet who has not been a shepherd." The desert was the site for the incubation of a great soul, in quietness and contemplation. He passed his days thinking the long, long thoughts of youth. This sort of thing still happens.

The head of personnel for the Foreign Mission Board spoke to our pastor's group recently. He indicated that the vast majority of mission volunteers come from rural and mountain areas, not from urban centers where Southern Baptists are strong. No one is quite sure why this is so.

Moses had to be a man for great patience. He waited, living in the desert for forty years before the call came. This can be such a hard lesson to learn. Impatience is the mark of immaturity. Jesus waited until he was thirty to begin his ministry. Paul spent three years in a desert retreat before beginning his missionary work. Moses' "weapons were tempered." He had time to sort out the truth, until it became as clear as the desert air.

## The Gaze of Wonder (vv. 2-3)

A bush afire in the desert may not have been an uncommon sight. There was scant vegetation and months without rain. A shrub could become as dry as tinder and burn in a puff of smokeless flame. The unique thing about the bush Moses saw was that it burned without being consumed. Interpreters have offered various explanations. Perhaps the bush was over a crevice in the rock where natural gas seeped out. It could have been a type of St. Elmo's fire or foxfire (phosphorous)—but that is seen only in the dark. If you visit the monastery at Mt. Sinai the monks have a bush with bright red leaves which they call the burning bush. Still others suggest that Moses' call experience was a vision, like Isaiah's.

But all these attempted explanations miss the point. The truth here is not how the bush burned, but the fact that God got Moses' attention, revealed himself to the shepherd, and called him to service. The important thing is not how it was done, but who caused it and why. Moses encountered God at the burning bush.

In calling Moses, God showed his concern for the oppressed:"I have seen . . . I have heard . . . I know the plight of my people" (Author's translation).

Moses' curiosity led to awe and worship. This is often the case. Many have gone out of curiosity to hear Billy Graham only to encounter the claim of God on their lives. Many a fellow who grew up in the country went to church to see the girls and found faith. Some who come to scoff, remain to pray. Larry Flynt recently cited his conversion, that of Chuck Colsen and Johnny Cash. Then he said, "God must have a sense of humor!"

## The Angel of the Lord (vv. 4-5)

The angel of the Lord appeared in the shape of a flame of fire from the burning bush. This was a theophany or appearance of God. The angels were God's messengers.

Moses' experience was a call to reverence. The shepherd was told to remove his shoes, for the ground on which he stood was holy. Here we see an encounter between holy God and sinful man. Great mystery surrounds the Almighty. We are not to be cozy with him. God is eternal and we are mortal; God is wise and we are ignorant in so many areas;

God is powerful and we are limited. He is *Mysterium Tremendum*—great mystery.

Today, when entering a mosque, you remove your shoes as a sign of respect for the holy place. Moses took off his shoes to worship and rolled his sleeves up to work. Both are necessary.

"I am the God of your father, the God of Abraham, the God of Isaac, and the God of Jacob" (v. 6), said the voice from the burning bush. This was no new deity. There was continuity in the call of Moses with the call of Abraham. Yahweh was the same God. Even so, our faith is built on the faith of our fathers. It becomes new to us in our day. We are the heirs of all Christian history.

## Moses' Call to Service

He was called to no easy task. He was to forge a nation from a slave gang; to codify a new law; and to found a new religion. Though the assignment was a tough one, and Moses was reluctant, God promised to go with him. Moses made repeated excuses, but God answered them. Moses was no volunteer—he was drafted.

God is *calling* still:

> Earth's crammed with heaven,
> And every common bush afire with God;
> But only he who sees, takes off his shoes.

Christians are being called to service today. We are not simply called to faith. We are also called to an ethical life-style and to mission. We are all ministers, with a unique ministry for God, touching lives no other believer may touch. You have been called by God and are now being set apart to the gospel ministry. Be sensitive to human need and hurt. Be ready to share your faith. Look for an opportunity to witness.

Within the next few years, there will come calls for service in the Volunteer Mission Corps. There will be a need for 2,500 foreign mission and 2,500 home mission volunteers. They will be asked to give one or two years of mission service, with the local church paying their living expenses.

God is calling still; calling to ministry; calling to missions. You have heard his call to ministry and responded, "Here am I, Lord. Send me." May you always be open to his call. May God bless you in your ministry to persons for him.

# A GLORIOUS PRESUMPTION

by C. Welton Gaddy

Ordination is one of the church's glorious presumptions. It should never be taken either too lightly or too seriously. It must not be taken too lightly because it is one means of response to God's call to minister. However, it should never be taken too seriously because it is an act of men.

No sudden magical transformation takes place during an act of ordination. If the one who comes to that hour is not a minister of the gospel already called by God, he will not be such when the service is over. Spiritually speaking, the laying on of hands no more makes one a minister than the ceremonial exchange of wedding bands binds two persons in a marriage. Ordination is not an act which makes one any better morally or any more authoritative spiritually though it should come as a recognition of previously demonstrated spiritual authority and authentic morality.

Ordination is an act of men. The old question which invariably used to be voiced by ordination councils makes a good point. The candidate was asked: "What would you do if we failed to ordain you?" The expected answer was, "I would go on preaching. I would go on ministering anyway." The insight was that ordination does not give legitimacy to the gospel ministry nearly so much as it gives recognition to this ministry. The boundaries of what God is doing in this world through his people are certainly not marked by ordination.

All of this is not to suggest that ordination is unimportant. That would be a serious mistake. Ordination is extremely important. When a person experiences the call of God to channel life in a special form of ministry, it is important that the church officially recognize this. As a particular congregation moves to ordain one of its number, it goes on record as rejoicing with this person that God's special call has been heard and accepted.

Thus, ordination is an act of affirmation. In current youth parlance, it's like the church saying, "Right on, Brother." This act of recognition is beneficial both to the church and to the ordained. For the church it is a word of encouragement concerning the nature of its life—it has been a place where one could hear the call of God and follow his divine leadership. For the person ordained, it is an act of confirmation. These people have recognized my response to God's call. Now as I confirm my acceptance of God's call, they are confirming their confidence in this relationship and offering to stand with me in my response.

This suggests another factor which is involved in ordination. It is a commitment on the part of those doing the ordaining. Anytime the church ordains a minister or a deacon it commits itself to intercessory support on that person's behalf, not the least of which is intercessory prayer. An unwritten pledge is made to support the ministry of the person in any way support is needed. The ordained may function in that particular congregation or go out from their midst—either way the weight of the congregation's support is to be felt. Prayers for the person are not to cease even as other visible means of support are to continue.

## Significance

The question is often raised as to how the work of the ordained is to differ from the work of any other Christian within the church. The theological answer is that there is little difference. Any person who calls Christ "Lord" has the responsibility to be about ministry in his name. Practically, however, there are some differences. Not every person can give full-time attention to a church vocation. Not all even have the particular gifts that are needed in church leadership. Thus, ordination sets apart those to whom God has given the necessary gifts of church leadership; those who have experienced God's call to spend the entirety of life utilizing these gifts in relation to the church.

Make no mistake though, ordination is not a means by which a congregation relinquishes any responsibilities for ministry which it may have. Ordination is not a process of designating or assigning responsibilities for ministers as the work of one person. In fact, the congregation which ordains one of its members invites a deeper understanding of its responsibilities as well as concrete suggestions of how to carry out these responsibilities.

In the New Testament, the church leader is the enabler. The minister does not act on behalf of the congregation in ministering to peoples' needs. Rather, the minister helps the members of the congregation know better how to effectively meet each other's needs in ministry as well as those of persons outside the church.

Christian ordination for the ministry is narrow in the sense that it is for only one ministry—the gospel ministry. It is broad in the sense that this one ministry may take many forms.

## Proclamation

What is the ministry of the gospel? That's an important question, for the gospel ministry is that with which all Christians are charged and yet to which some are called in a special way. As I understand it, the gospel ministry is the process by which one brings the gospel into interaction with all of life. Look closely at what this involves.

The content of the gospel is a person—Jesus Christ—who meets persons with an invitation and a demand. The minister of Christ is one who both by words and deeds sounds the inviting and demanding Word made flesh in Jesus.

The first word of this minister is a positive inviting word. He relates what God has done and what this means for the person in need. Whether by sermon, song, counsel, presence, or whatever, that which is conveyed is compassion and that which is offered is a relationship.

- The lost are confronted by a person so loving as to invite confession, the prelude to forgiveness. They are invited toward the experience of salvation.
- Those at war with themselves are made to feel accepted and offered a transforming peace.
- Those who have looked death in the face and grown frantic with fear are made aware of an abiding presence and invited to begin experiencing eternal life with One who will never leave them—not even in the "valley of the shadow."
- Those who have felt trapped by life and weighted down with decision making are lovingly invited to experience an unbelievable quality of freedom and to accept the gift of divine wisdom.

It is little wonder that the biblical writer got so carried away and said, "How beautiful are the feet of those who bring good news—gospel."

## Service

Such are the first words and the first acts of gospel ministry. They are positive, upbuilding, supportive, redemptive.

The gospel ministry does not end at that point. Demand follows invitation. Challenge accompanies comfort. Comprehensive evangelism is important, but so is Christian nurture. To win persons to Christ without helping them mature in their newfound faith is to produce a generation of full-grown Christians with the spiritual mentality of babies. This represents an inadequate view of the ministry as well as a sin against the church. One who is ordained is charged with doing the *whole* gospel.

Where there is blessing, there is responsibility. Where there is opportunity, there is demand. The gospel ministry involves translating the confession of Christ as Lord into specific acts demonstrative of the lordship. The minister can never forget in his witness or his own personal life the demands which the lordship of Christ makes on the lives of people in terms of both their private and social responsibilities.

Teaching becomes as important as preaching. Practical example becomes as important as the proclamation of lofty ideals.

On March 16, 1960, when Chancellor Konrad Adenauer was visiting in Washington, Lyndon Johnson, who was then a senator, asked him, "What would you say if you were asked to say one thing to the American people?"

The answer came quickly, "Educate your children. No price is too precious to pay for education. And by education, I mean moral education, too. May I speak frankly?" the Chancellor continued.

"Of course," answered Johnson.

"I have never seen as great a lack of moral integrity as I have among your young people. I do not believe that in the conflict between East and West the young people of the free world have the moral integrity to win." Obviously, the same thing could have been said about our adults.

There is the challenge for the ordained. Translate faith into moral terms to make belief convincing in behavior. Revealed religion has always been relative religion and the relevancy of Christianity is to be both proclaimed and demonstrated in the life of the minister.

Thus, through speaking, singing, praying, or whatever, the minister may address a matter of personal morality such as the evil of dependence upon drugs whether they be alcohol, which is the chief cause of drug problems, or other drugs; the importance of honest speech and a vocabulary that is not polluted; or a matter of social morality such as integrity in government and the importance of Christians being good citizens; economic justice and a view of stewardship that makes one responsible for the 90 percent not tithed; the necessity of eradicating prejudice and working in racial equality. You see, the gospel ministry is as broad as all of life, for it is infiltrating all of life with the person of Christ.

We need that; the church needs that; the world needs that. Our world is in a mess. Some people need desperately to confess their sins and receive forgiveness and salvation.

Some people who have been stagnant Christians for years on end need to begin to grow in their faith and understand its application for life.

All need what the gospel has to offer and demand.

What a powerful spiritual allegory is the story told in the *Poseidon Adventure*. In the midst of frantic cries for help and chaotic behavior, one man had the wisdom and the courage to point out a way of escape. Not all would listen, but to a world turned upside down he said there is only one way out, and he pointed to a Christmas tree.

I don't want to oversimplify, but I believe if our world is to be saved, there must be those who point out the way of escape from chaos and the way of entrance into life eternal. It can only happen as they point us Godward by pointing us to Christ. That is why all of those who are called to the gospel ministry need the recognition, support, and prayer which comes with ordination.

## Love

Oh, you may say, that is most presumptuous. It is presumptuous for the church to feel that it can find anyone who will attempt to be so responsible. It is presumptuous for any person to accept ordination with its blessing and responsibility. You may think that presumptuous. I think you're right. But that, my friends has been throughout the history of the church and must now be in the present hour our glorious presumption.

# An Ordination Sermon Prototype

## CALLED TO PREACH

by William E. Hull

When Paul argued with the Epicurean and Stoic philosophers in Athens, some of them voiced the question which congregations still ask every time a preacher stands to speak, "What will this babbler say?" (Acts 17:18). There is no better way for us to answer the query than with an affirmation of the great apostle: "We preach not ourselves, but Christ Jesus the Lord" (2 Cor. 4:5).

## We Preach

Why did Paul say, "We preach"? His training as a rabbi was in synagogue argumentation rather than in gospel proclamation (Acts 22:3). The itinerant philosophers of Greece and Rome were not preachers, nor were the apocalyptic sectarians of Palestine. Indeed, there was a dearth of preaching in Paul's day. Most people either looked back to the golden age of prophecy which had ended centuries earlier with the collection of its sacred writings, or they looked forward to its revival in a final age at the end of history.

No, Paul did not define his role from the religious fashions of his time but from the nature of the Christian movement into which he had been thrust by the call of his Lord. Jesus, like his forerunner John, had "come preaching" (Matt. 3:1; 4:17), thereby breaking the silence of the centuries. So well did he train his first followers that the launching of the church at Pentecost was essentially an explosion of preaching, the gift of a new tongue to address all mankind with the gospel as the Spirit gave utterance (Acts 2:4).[1] Long before Christianity had any institutions, organizations, or even the New Testament writings, it lived and grew by its preaching. It may well be that the seeds of conversion were planted in Paul's life through the fearless sermon of Stephen which was sealed by his martyrdom (cf. Acts 7:58; 9:4).

The letters of Paul reflect again and again his keen awareness that at best, preaching is a precarious, even scandalous, business. For this kind of declaration depends neither on the wisdom of its substance (as with philosophy), nor on the cleverness of its structure (as with debate), nor on the elegance of its style (as with oratory). This is why, in a profound discussion of his preaching in the early chapters of 1 Corinthians, Paul frankly admitted that for most of his hearers, whether they be Jew or Greek, preaching was "folly" (1:18, RSV).

The scandal of preaching is still with us today. A good case can again be made that its golden age lies in the past. Even in the last century F. W. Robertson lamented the decline of the pulpit with these words: "By the change of times the pulpit has lost its place. It does only part of that whole which used to be done by it alone. Once it was newspaper, schoolmaster, theological treatise, a stimulant to good works, historical lecture, metaphysics, etc., all in one."[2] Now there are a multitude of competing authorities—scientists, journalists, psychiatrists, even the ubiquitous radio and television commentators.

Let us candidly confront this chilling claim that the pulpit is no longer the prow of the church, much less of civilization, as Herman Melville visualized it in *Moby Dick.* Ask any pulpit committee after months of intensive investigation and travel: How many pastors in the Southern Baptist Convention are even trying to build their careers on the centrality of preaching? Instead, reputations are more often made through promotional techniques (ecclesiastical gimmickry), advertising skills, political adroitness, and a host of inferior substitutes. Subtle but excruciating pressures are brought to bear on the minister today to spend all of the week feverishly engineering some spectacular scheme designed to draw attention to his church, then on Saturday night to dust off somebody else's clever sermon outline (semantic gimmickry) for use the next morning.

Against that swift-running tide, I have come to this conference to reassert the enduring primacy of preaching. After twenty years of constant visitation in every kind of church imaginable, it is my conviction that preaching more than any other ministerial activity sets the tone of congregational life. To be sure, a Sunday morning soliloquy is no substitute for personal counseling or committee meetings, but I would observe that trivial preaching quickly trivializes these essential weekday endeavors. Paul Tillich was right in his contention that religion is nothing if it is not "ultimate concern,"[3] and urgent preaching is the wellspring of that seriousness which must pervade all that a church does. Turn the sermon into nothing more than a jingle of artificially alliterated phrases augmented by pious moralisms drawn from *Reader's Digest,* and soon the curse of blandness will settle like a choking cloud of dust over the entire enterprise.

But some cry that preaching is a "sitting-down exercise" which easily becomes a substitute for action. The point is well taken, but note that one must first make the point (that is, preach a sermon on it) before anything is done about it. More, note that to say the needed word of rebuke to our apathy may in itself be the most courageous act possible. How many centuries did mankind wait for somebody to speak up and say that sweatshops and slavery and segregation were wrong? How many more centuries must pass before we learn to say with equal clarity that war, poverty, and oppression are also wrong? In each case, fearless action will be required, but the word is essential prerequisite to the deed. Only when we find our tongues are we able, with a web of words, to weave together our isolated interests into that community of united concern which is the only instrument of effective social change.

There is more than editorial modesty in the pronoun "we preach." The plural points to the solidarity of the people of God in one shared proclamation. Preaching is no isolated one-on-one encounter. Rather, it is the crucible in which authentic fellowship is formed. Speech itself is the most social act of which we are capable. When that speech voices the one true gospel, then all who hear receive a gift in common which reconciles their fragmentation caused by the babel of earthly tongues (Gen. 11:1-9).

In the strength of that bond by which we all cling to one common word, there is help for the inner crisis of meaning. We really do not need more deeds to do; our lives are already full of constant activity. Rather, we need to discover a dimension of significance to the harried pace of the daily round. For instance: "My best friend died of leukemia last week at age forty-two—what does it mean?" "The courts integrated my child's school last week—what does it mean?" "A leader in our church was divorced last week—what does it mean?"

James Russell Lowell wrote eloquently of this "transfiguring" function of preaching when he described the lectures of Ralph Waldo Emerson. "We used to listen," said he, "to that thrilling voice of his, so charged with subtle music, as shipwrecked men on a raft to the hail of a ship that came with unhoped-for food and rescue." Why? "The delight and the benefit were that he put us in communication with a larger style of thought ... gave us ravishing glimpses of an ideal under the dry husk of our New

England; made us conscious of the supreme and everlasting originality of whatever bit of soul might be in any of us; freed us, in short, from the stocks of prose in which we had sat so long that we had grown well-nigh contented in our cramps." Then Lowell asked and answered the key question: "Did our own imaginations transfigure dry remainder-bisquit into ambrosia? At any rate, he brought us life, which on the whole, is no bad thing."[4]

## "Not Ourselves"

Strange that Paul should inject this negation into the center of our text. For he, more than anyone, had much to preach about himself (2 Cor. 6:3-10): a dramatic conversion (Acts 9:1-19; 22:3-21; 26:4-23); impressive evangelistic results (Acts 13:4-12; 16:25-34); heroic missionary service (2 Cor. 11:22-28); and remarkable heavenly visions (2 Cor. 12:1-4). Indeed, would we not consider ourselves fortunate to be able to sit all day and listen to Paul preach on his amazing exploits?

Moreover, we know that the opponents of the apostle were certainly preaching about themselves (2 Cor. 11:12-21). One group, the Judaizers, were boasting of the laws they kept, of the circumcision they had undergone, of the festivals which they had observed (Gal. 1:6-9; 4:10; 5:7-12). Another group, the Gnostics, were proud of their special knowledge, of their separation from ordinary people, of their resurrection out of the mundane world (1 Cor. 3:18-21; 4:8-13; 5:9-11). Yet a third group, the original followers and relatives of Jesus, were making much of their participation in the earthly ministry of the Lord and hence of their foundational status in the life of the church (Gal. 1:11 to 2:10). On every side Paul was sorely tempted to outshine the claims of his adversaries by preaching about himself, but he steadfastly refused.

Why? Because Paul realized that the proper subject matter of the gospel could never be man, any man, even himself. Nothing he had done provided any basis for proclamation. After all, he was the "chief of sinners" (1 Tim. 1:15). The apostle realized that, more often than not, true preaching is in spite of, rather than because of, its spokesmen (Phil. 1:15-18). For the subject matter of the gospel is God. Its plot is the story of Jesus. Its validation is the power of the Holy Spirit. Preaching is not a recital of what man has done for God but what God has done for man! It is not a proclamation about the power of God but is that divine power at work for human redemption (Rom. 1:16). The preacher's utterance is not an informed opinion on spiritual issues. Rather it is a divine occurrence in which the Christ-event actually happens all over again.[5] This does not mean that confessional preaching is not valid. What it means, rather, is that our testimony concerns the object of the gospel, not the subject of the gospel.

How strange that in the face of this fundamental distinction, the motto of many pulpits today might well read, "We preach ourselves." That is not a charge of ministerial egotism or of homiletical self-centeredness. Rather, many preachers, recoiling from massive criticisms lodged against the ancient message, are openly insisting that they have only themselves to preach. There is no longer any certainty in the "prescientific" views of Scripture now two thousand and more years old. Even theology was formulated in concepts that are obsolete. The terminology of yesterday is said to have lost its potency in speaking to the sophisticated intellectuals of today. The last retreat for the preacher, therefore, is to take his stand behind the bulwark of his own experience.

Many factors have contributed to this self-conscious religious humanism in the pulpit. Philosophically, existentialism has nourished a passionate introspection which sets the subjectivities of the immediate and the inward above the objectivities of the ancient and the external. Psychologically, the pastoral care movement has stressed clinical data from autobiographical reflections as the basis for religious awareness. Culturally, the sense of modernity has been so overpoweringly strong that many theologians have subordinated their gospels to the dominant intellectual current of the day. On every hand we see evidence that Western scientific empiricism is being yoked to Eastern mystical privatism to reinforce the assumption that nothing is real and true unless we have experienced it for ourselves.

It is not surprising, therefore, to observe that the calling which Paul described as a "scandal," and which got him labeled as a "fool," has in our day become instead a cult of heroes. For once we begin to "preach ourselves," then those with the most fascinating selves have the most to say. They may be beauty queens, or All-American athletes, or reformed politicians, or media entertainers. Nor is there anything wrong with these achievements as such. In fact, religiously there is nothing either good or bad about such credentials, since they are really quite irrelevant, which means that ordinary preachers need to be neither contemptuous nor jealous nor deferential to these overnight stars who suddenly steal the pulpit limelight. The real problem with the celebrity approach to preaching is rather that because of all the ballyhoo most people will come to hear them "preach themselves" even though some of them may sincerely attempt to do better.

James Denney was right when he said: "No man can give at once the impression that he himself is clever and that Jesus Christ is mighty to save."[6]

Why is it so crucial to emphasize that what we preach is "not ourselves"? In part because that sharp negation sets the scandal of the gospel in proper perspective. There are controversial themes in the Bible that we preachers would just as soon not touch. Left to ourselves, we might be tempted to choose safety and serenity by muting or ignoring these dangerous issues. But that is just the point: We do not preach ourselves (our preferences and priorities). Rather, we preach a Word that is fire in our mouths (Jer. 5:14), that is bitter to our stomachs (Rev. 10:9-11). It is a Word that we may quake to speak as much as our listeners may quake to hear. It is a Word that may judge us more severely than it does them. But it is a Word that cannot be denied, not because we want to be cantankerous, but because, quite simply, we are not in control of our pulpit agenda. As Hugh Thompson Kerr put it, "We are ambassadors not diplomats."[7]

## "But Jesus Christ as Lord"

That being so, what, then, are we to preach? Paul had his answer ready: "Jesus Christ as Lord." The name "Jesus" identified a life and ministry lived out in Palestine for a few short years around AD 30. The title "Christ" pointed to the meaning of that life and ministry as fulfilling all the hopes of Israel anticipated in Holy Scripture. But the appellation "Lord" meant that this fulfillment was no isolated achievement limited to one place or time; rather, it asserted the supremacy of this Jesus the Messiah over the totality of human existence in every age.

It was no easier for Paul to preach "Jesus Christ as Lord" in his day than for us to do so in ours. He had not participated in the earthly ministry of Jesus and so was at a disadvantage in preaching to the Jews who had. He knew that the messianic claims implied by the title Christ were viewed as narrowly nationalistic and so held in contempt among the Greeks to whom he preached. And he knew that Caesar was murderously hostile to any rival who would claim the status of Lord among the Romans to whom he preached. Despite every difficulty, however, this is what Paul was determined to preach. This message alone declared that his Savior was not only the climax to all human history but also the clue to all human hopes, and the comfort to all human hurts. It was also the cosmic potentate of the entire universe. To affirm anything less would have compromised the uniqueness and finality of his redemptive work.

By comparison, what midget claims we make for our Master today. How seldom do we hear preaching that sets Jesus as the centerpiece of history, that views his life as the apex of Old Testament revelation, that installs his authority above that of political, economic, and ideological rulers of the present age. In his spiritual autobiography *A Sort of Life,* Graham Greene quotes Flaubert: "Human language is like a cracked kettle on which we beat out the tunes for bears to dance to, when all the time we are longing to move the stars to pity."[8] Too much of our preaching lies under that curse of blandness. We suppose that we have gotten results when we see a lot of action, but often it is nothing more than the bears dancing to our pulpit tunes while the great shaping forces of life, the stars that guide human destiny, remain unmoved by our trivial rhetoric.

Let us not mount the pulpit to debate peripheral questions or to speculate on esoteric curiosities. We are not put there to haunt the sideshows of life or to substitute fanciful theories for the eternal gospel. We are there to preach Jesus Christ as Lord.

In a profound sense, one of the greatest conflicts in our century, World War II, was a war of words. It all began when a fanatical paperhanger named Adolf Hitler used spellbinding speeches to rally a broken nation with visions of conquest and glory. Soon his frenzied oratory had whipped Germany into a military juggernaut which quickly brought Europe to its knees. Across a narrow channel lay the last holdout, with Winston Churchill at its helm. Reeling under the blows of Nazi aggression, England committed every plane to its skies, every boat to its shores, every able-bodied man to defend its streets; but even that valiant effort was not enough.

With disaster staring him in the face, Churchill took up the weapon of his adversary and began to do battle with words. From a concrete bombshelter deep underground, he spoke to the people of Britain not of superiority but of sacrifice, not of conquest but of courage, not of revenge but of renewal.

Slowly but surely, Winston Churchill talked England back to life. To beleaguered old men waiting on their rooftops with buckets of water for the fire bombs to land, to frightened women and children huddled behind sandbags with sirens screaming overhead, to exhausted pilots dodging tracer bullets in the midnight sky, his words not only announced a new dawn but also conveyed the strength to bring it to pass.

No wonder Ruskin described a sermon as "thirty minutes to raise the dead."[9] That is our awesome assignment: to put into deeds the new day that is ours in Jesus Christ our Lord.

The preceding address was given by William E. Hull at the National Conference on Preaching, Ingleside Baptist Church, Shreveport, Louisiana, April 3, 1978. It may be adapted for use as an ordination sermon. Dr. Hull is pastor of the First Baptist Church of Shreveport.

[1] See Amos N. Wilder, *The Language of the Gospel: Early Christian Rhetoric* (New York: Harper & Row, 1964), pp. 9-25.

[2] A. Brooke Stopford, editor, *Life and Letters of Frederick W. Robertson* (Boston: Ticknor and Fields, 1865), vol. II, pp. 59-60. Cited by Kyle Haselden, *The Urgency of Preaching* (New York: Harper & Row, 1963), p. 16.

[3] Paul Tillich, *Systematic Theology* (Chicago: University of Chicago Press, 1967), three volumes in one. See all references under "ultimate concern" in the Index to vol. III, p. 442.

[4] James Russell Lowell, *The Nation*, 1868.

[5] See William E. Hull, "The Glory of the Gospel" (Shreveport Sermons #77, Part II).

[6] Quoted by James S. Stewart, *Heralds of God* (New York: Charles Scribner's Sons, 1964), p. 74.

[7] Quoted in *Christianity Today*, January 19, 1962, p. 3.

[8] Cited in *Time*, September 27, 1971, p. 94.

[9] Cited by Donald G. Miller, *Fire in Thy Mouth* (New York: Abingdon, 1954), p. 17.

## LITANY OF RESPONSE
## DEACON ORDINATION

Pastor: We are gathered tonight to worship God and to ordain our
brothers in Christ, _____
_____, _____,
servants of the Lord as deacons.

**People: We gladly and joyfully set them apart for this high
office.**

Pastor: Serving as a deacon is more than just an honor; it is a task
which calls for service, faithfulness, humility, openness,
courage to speak and live one's convictions.

**People: Through our knowledge of them we have found that
they possess these traits.**

Pastor: As a member of the diaconate, they will be charged with
guiding our church to reach people for Christ and to train
them in Christian discipleship.

**People: We will seek to follow their leading so that our
church may accomplish this goal.**

Candidates: We will willingly serve God and his Son Jesus Christ through
this church, but we must have your support and cooperation.

**People: We offer you our support and pledge our help in every
way that it is possible to give.**

Candidates: Will you give serious consideration to ways in which our
church can be faithful and creative in being the body of
Christ in this community?

**People: We pledge that we will take seriously our call to
establish a Christlike presence in this community
and will support you in doing so.**

Candidates: We accept this pledge of support and will to the best of our
spiritual awareness, strive to be worthy of this trust and of the
name Deacon.

**Pastor: I pledge you my assistance, openness, cooperation,
and initiative so that together we can magnify our
Lord and Savior, Jesus Christ.**

Candidates: We are willing to join with you in serving to accomplish the
goals of the church and not to further selfish ends.

119

Deacons: As those deacons with whom you will be serving, we welcome you into our body and pray that God will bless you, our church, and us as we are faithful to him.

**Congregation: We ask our heavenly Father to guide faithfully our church and these men who lead us.**

Pastor: May our one goal be to proclaim Jesus Christ so that all may come to know his love.

**All: "Let us not be weary in well-doing: for in due season we shall reap, if we faint not."**

# Deacon Ordination Sermons

## DEACONS—THOSE WHO SERVE

by Alton H. McEachern

Deacons, likewise, must be men of high principle, not indulging in double talk, given neither to excessive drinking nor to money-grubbing. They must be men who combine a clear conscience with a firm hold on the deep truths of our faith. No less than bishops, they must first undergo a scrutiny, and if there is no mark against them, they may serve. Their wives, equally, must be women of high principle, who will not talk scandal, sober and trustworthy in every way. A deacon must be faithful to his one wife, and good at managing his children and his own household. For deacons with a good record of service may claim a high standing and the right to speak openly on matters of the Christian faith (1 Tim. 3:8-13, NEB).

In the New Testament church there were three groups of spiritual leaders. The first of these were the *apostoloi* or apostles. The word means "one sent" and includes the original twelve disciples and others such as the apostle Paul. The modern equivalent is a missionary.

The second group of leaders were called by two titles in the early church. They were called *episcopoi* or bishops. The word means an overseer. The other word is *presbuteros* or elder. Both these terms were used to describe the pastor or shepherd of the flock.

A third category of spiritual leaders were called *diakanos* or deacons. This word means "one who serves." The qualifications for deacons are almost identical to those given for pastors in 1 Timothy 3:1-7. Note the specific qualifications:

## The Deacon's Character (v. 8)

The deacon is to be a person of integrity. He should be thoughtful and capable of making decisions—not scatterbrained.

"Not indulging in double talk" (NEB). The Greek means speaking with two voices. Perhaps this is what the American Indian means by "speaking with a forked tongue." Clarence Jordan's translation says that deacons should be "straight shooters."

The deacon is not to be "given to much wine" or "excessive drinking"

(NEB). A deacon is to be a person of self-control and not overindulgent.

A deacon should not be greedy for money. He is to earn his living honestly and to set an example as a good steward of his financial resources. Moffatt translates this term "not pilfering" or honest. The deacon's character and integrity are to be above question.

## The Deacon's Faith (v. 9)

A deacon is to have "a firm hold on the deep truths of our faith." He is to know Christ firsthand, as a regenerate believer. He should be able to share his faith naturally. As an upright person he is to hold the faith "with a clear conscience."

## The Deacon's Probation (v. 10)

Let the deacon "first be proved" and not a new convert. Persons to be ordained as deacons should be a member of the church long enough that the congregation will have ample opportunity to judge their spiritual sincerity and gifts.

## "The Women" (v. 11)

Two translations are possible here. It may refer to qualifications for the deacon's wife, or for deaconesses (female deacons). In the early church female deacons instructed women candidates for baptism and ministered to needs of women members of the congregation. Phoebe is cited in Romans 16:1 as a deaconess.

Ordinarily, the qualifications listed here are applied to the deacon's wife. She is to be supportive of her husband and the church, and is to be equally well qualified as her husband. Deacons' wives are to be women of high principle. They should be temperate, persons of "discretion and self-control" (Phillips). Deacons' wives are not to be gossips, confidence repeaters, or slanderers. They are to be trustworthy in every way; faithful in all things. They will be loyal to Christ and the church. In the New Testament church, women were given new dignity and responsibilities. This was radical in the first-century world.

## "A One Woman Man" (v. 12)

A deacon is to be faithful to his one wife. This was probably a prohibition against polygamy as well as the selection of a remarried divorcée. The deacon is to set a high standard in morality and family life.

The deacon is to manage his children and household well. Thus, he demonstrates that he can lead in the church which is the family of God.

## The Deacon's Reward (v. 13)

Deacons who serve well attain a high standing in the community of faith. They receive the respect and honor of their fellow believers. And they gain great confidence in the faith, "the right to speak openly on matters of the Christian faith" (NEB).

We do not know the names or biographies of all the deacons in the New Testament church. However, two of these men were very prominent. Stephen was a preaching deacon who became the first Christian to climb the martyr's steep ascent into glory. He was stoned, because of his faith and witness, outside the city wall of Jerusalem (see Acts 6:8-10). Another early deacon was Philip. He was an effective witness to his faith and was greatly used of the Lord. (Read about him in Acts 8:26-40.)

J. Winston Pearce tells about a boy who was asked to define a deacon. He said, "A deacon is something you set on fire and put on a hill."

There are similarities between a deacon and a beacon. The challenge to deacons is: Be a beacon for Christ in your church and community, as "one who serves."

## Stephen and Philip Set the Example:

A Biblical Basis for Witnessing Deacons

by Alton H. McEachern

Have you ever wondered about a deacon's qualifications and responsibilities?

The New Testament provides the qualifications for deacons (see 1 Tim. 3:8-13). It also tells about the origin of the office (Acts 6:1-7). Acts 6—8 gives us a case study of two New Testament deacons in action. Deacons Stephen and Philip dominate the narrative in these three chapters. They stand out as mighty witnesses to their faith. The example of these men gives a biblical basis for modern deacons to become effective witnesses in their church and community. As we consider the activities of Stephen and Philip, we will discover three characteristics common to both: (1) Each knew and used the Scriptures. (2) Each was Spirit-filled and Spirit-led. (3) Each was a mighty witness to his Lord.

This passage marks the beginning of missions in Christian history.

## Seven Good Men

A problem arose in the Jerusalem church. Widows of Greek origin in the congregation felt neglected in the distribution of benevolence. It was important to meet human need, but the apostles felt distracted from their preaching and teaching task by this practical problem. They called a congregational meeting and recommended that the church select seven good men who could take on this administrative duty. The spiritual qualifications of the seven were carefully spelled out: They should be men of good reputation, men who were filled with the Spirit, and men who were wise. These highly respected leaders were to be both spiritual and practical—not a bad combination.

The church was pleased with the apostles' suggestion and elected seven men. They all had Greek names. Stephen, the first named and most prominent, may have been their chairman. The seven were ordained with prayer and by the laying on of hands by the apostles (6:6).

The results of electing these first seven deacons were measurable and exciting! The Word of God was more effectively proclaimed, and the number of believers "multiplied in Jerusalem greatly" (6:7).

## Stephen, a Powerful Witness

This influential leader in Jerusalem church had a significant, if short-lived, career. His mighty witness to the faith attracted the enmity of Jewish leaders and precipitated a public debate. When Stephen got the best of them, they instigated false witnesses to charge him with blasphemy "against Moses and God." He was arrested and brought before the Sanhedrin (the Jewish religious supreme court). Stephen gave a brilliant defense of his faith before the council.

Stephen knew the Scriptures. Indeed, he traced the history of God's dealings with his people Israel. He cited the faith experience of Abraham and the other patriarchs: Isaac, Jacob, and Joseph. Then he told of the Hebrews' bondage in Egypt and their prayers for deliverance. Stephen recalled the life and work of Moses whom his enemies said he had blasphemed. He went on to tell about God's prophets and how they had been rejected, persecuted, and killed.

This was more than Stephen's enemies could stand. They became enraged and "ground their teeth against him" (7:54, RSV). They refused to hear his message, took him outside the city, and stoned him to death.

Stoning was the Jewish method of execution. The Romans used crucifixion. There is question as to whether the Jews had the *right* to use capital punishment. This scene is more a lynching than an official execution.

Thus, a deacon became the first Christian martyr. His death was not in vain; for as Tertullian, an early church leader, noted, the blood of martyrs became the seed of the church. It is interesting to note that the Greek word for martyr means "witness." Martyrdom is the supreme witness to one's faith. Deacon Stephen bore that ultimate testimony.

Stephen was a Spirit-filled deacon. The author of Acts makes this fact abundantly clear. When Stephen was elected as one of the seven, he was called "a man full of faith and of the Holy Spirit" (6:5, RSV). As Stephen gave his defense before the council, his face was aglow (6:15). At his martyrdom he was "full of the Holy Spirit" and was given a vision of the risen Christ standing at the right hand of God (7:55-56, RSV). Stephen showed the Spirit of Christ as he prayed for those who were killing him (7:60).

Note that Saul, the church's most severe persecutor, kept the coats of those who stoned Stephen and agreed with their action. The witness and prayer of this dying deacon must have been a crucial factor in the conversion of the enemy who would one day become the missionary apostle Paul. Deacons today may not be called literally to lay down their lives as a witness to Christ. However, they have the clear and brave example of Stephen in life as well as death.

## Philip, a Preaching Deacon

Following the execution of Stephen, a fierce persecution of the church broke out in Jerusalem. It was led by Saul who had held the coats of the mob and consented to Stephen's death. The believers were scattered. Most of them left Jerusalem (except the apostles themselves). They went everyplace preaching the Word. This scattering of believers represented the first missionary movement in the history of the young church. The result was that the movement spread like wildfire.

One of those who fled was deacon Philip. He went north to Samaria and proclaimed Christ (see 8:4-8). His message was met with a glad reception among the despised Samaritans whom the Jews considered halfbreeds and religious outcasts. However, the Samaritans were also looking forward to the coming of the Messiah, and they welcomed Philip's message. The results of Philip's witness were that many believed in Jesus as Messiah, many were healed, and there was great joy. He spoke about Jesus as naturally as we speak about our family, our hobbies, or our work. Modern deacons should speak naturally about their faith as well.

Real revival broke out in Samaria. There was great joy in that city. Both religious and racial barriers fell at the message of Christ.

Philip was a Spirit-led deacon. In the midst of great success, the Spirit led Philip to leave Samaria. He was told to go south toward Gaza (the ancient route to Egypt). He left a populated area to go into the desert. How strangely God seems to lead sometimes. Philip must have had some doubts about this leading.

Philip spoke Greek, the most universal language of that day. Thus, he was able to converse with this international prospect he encountered on the road to Gaza—an Ethiopian minister of state, the treasurer of his country. This eunuch was a God-fearer who had found spiritual truth in the religion of Israel. There he sat in his chariot (the equivalent of a modern limousine) reading Isaiah 53. Philip knew the Bible. He began at the prophecy of the Messiah and preached Christ to him. As the deacon opened the meaning of the Scripture to this powerful foreigner, the man believed. Philip explained the good news of Jesus Christ to the eunuch and at his request baptized him.

As Philip left, the Ethiopian went on his way rejoicing. The gospel brings joy. Tradition holds that this treasurer went home and evangelized Ethiopia. He couldn't keep this joy to himself. Imagine the joy Philip must have felt. He turned north from the town of Ashdod where he had encountered the Ethiopian and worked his way up the Mediterranean coast. Philip witnessed in each city until he came to the Roman capital, Caesarea. Do you suppose deacons today miss a lot of joy by failing to witness as they go?

Once a new convert came to Spurgeon, the London preacher. The man asked what he could do for Christ. Spurgeon asked what his work was. The convert replied that he was a railroad engineer.

"Is your fireman a Christian?" Spurgeon asked. When the engineer said he did not know, Spurgeon replied, "Well, find out, and begin by sharing your faith with him." Deacons can share their faith as Philip did—as they go.

These two first-century deacons were chosen for practical service in the church; however, their duties were not limited to administrative chores. They became powerful witnesses in Jerusalem and beyond. Recall the characteristics which they had in common:

- They were Spirit-filled deacons who were sensitive to God's leading.
- They knew the Scriptures and used them in sharing their faith.
- They bore a mighty witness. It leaped barriers of race and economic station. The results were far-reaching indeed. One convert carried the gospel to Africa, and another planted it in Europe.

Who knows how the Spirit might use our witness? Let us be sensitive to both his leading and to human spiritual needs.

# An Appendix:
# On the Ordination
# of Women

## The Ordination of Women

The question of the ordination of women is a lively topic of discussion within many denominations. Episcopalians have debated the issue. Pope John Paul II took a strong stand against the ordination of women priests during his visit to the United States in 1979.

Baptists differ in their opinions about the ordination of women as deacons and ministers. Those who favor and those who feel women should not be ordained are equally sincere. Both appeal to Scripture in supporting their positions. The Bible sets forth principles which speak to this question, but gives no specific instructions as to whether women should or should not be ordained. Indeed, as we saw in chapter 1, there is no clear mandate in the New Testament for the ordination of anyone. Still the roots for our ordination practice are found there.

In this brief appendix I have no illusion of changing anyone's viewpoint. But concerned Christians do need to examine the question in the light of biblical principles. It is my purpose to present both viewpoints on the ordination of women as deacons and ministers.

### The Role of Women in the New Testament

Women were quite prominent in the ministry of Jesus and in the life of the New Testament church. This is amazing in light of the status of women at that time. Jews, Greeks, and Romans had a low view of the woman's role. The Jews did not educate them, and women were not allowed to own property or give testimony in court. In worship they were relegated to an outer courtyard of the Temple or the balcony of a synagogue. The culture of the first century considered women the property of their father or husband.

## Women and the Ministry of Jesus

In the ministry of Jesus, women were "the first at the cradle and last at the cross." Indeed, it was a group of women who found Jesus' tomb empty on that first Easter morning and announced his resurrection. While Luke has been called "the women's Gospel," all the Evangelists show the prominence of women in Jesus' ministry. And this was in a time when most rabbis would not speak to a woman in public.

Luke begins with Mary's song called "the Magnificat," which is no "ho-hum" hymn. He records the visit of Mary and Elizabeth prior to the birth of Jesus and John the Baptist. Luke tells about Jesus raising a widow's son from the dead (7:11-17); healing Jairus's daughter and a woman who touched the hem of his garment (8:40-56). He also healed a woman on the sabbath (13:10-17). Jesus told a parable about a widow and commended another's generosity (18:1-8 and 21:1-4).

Luke told about a group of women who traveled with Jesus and supported his movement. He named three of them, Mary of Magdala, Joanna, and Suzanna (8:1-3). It was unusual to note the names of women. For example, Jesus' brothers were named in Scripture but not his sisters (Mark 6:3). The reader will recall Jesus' visits in the home of Mary, Martha, and Lazarus at Bethany; his encounter with a woman taken in adultery; and his conversation with the woman at the well in Samaria; as well as his anointing by still another woman.

The point is that Jesus treated women as persons of equal worth. He took them and their questions seriously. No act of Jesus, no parable he told was ever at the expense of women. He never made light of them. Jesus was the Liberator of all persons—men, women, and children.

## Women in the New Testament Church

In the New Testament era women played a prominent role in the life and ministry within the churches. Again this must have seemed radical in such a man's world. A group of widows carried out a significant deacon-type ministry in the early church (1 Tim. 5:3-16). Note the discussion of their role as well in Philippians 4:3. Lydia was a prominent leader in the church in Philippi.

The apostle Paul considered such women as Euodia, Syntyche, and

Priscilla, his "co-workers" in spreading the gospel (Phil. 4:2; Rom. 16:3). He called Phoebe a deaconess in Romans 16:1.

In Acts 21:9 Philip's four daughters are cited as inspired preachers. This appears to be a fulfillment of Joel's prophecy and the coming of the Holy Spirit on the New Testament church. This was a mark of the inbreaking of the messianic age. See Joel 2:28-32 and Acts 2:17-18, Simon Peter's sermon on the day of Pentecost: "This is what was spoken by the prophet Joel: 'And in the last days it shall be, God declares, that I will pour out my Spirit upon all flesh, and your sons and your daughters shall prophesy .... Yea, and on my menservants and my maidservants in those days I will pour out my Spirit; and they shall prophesy' "(RSV). In the New Testament a prophet was not a fortune-teller but an inspired preacher of the good news.

## Women in the Churches Today

As in the New Testament era, so today women are very much involved in the life and ministry of the churches. Most churches have a majority of women members. They, as well as baptized children within the church, have an equal vote in church conferences and congregational decision-making. Our polity makes a Baptist church a spiritual democracy. Most of our missionaries are women. They, too, have a full vote and voice in the governing annual "mission meeting."

In our churches women teach the Bible, take part in church music, and serve on church committees. Southern Baptists are indebted to the women for keeping our commitment to missions strong. Our two major annual offerings for foreign and home missions are named for Lottie Moon and Annie Armstrong.

Some Southern Baptist churches have ordained women as ministers. The total number currently is less than a hundred, and few of these serve as pastors. A growing number of women are enrolling in our six seminaries in the schools of theology as well as in religious education and church music.

More of our churches are reexamining the biblical materials and ordaining women as deacons. This has occurred in a number of states from Virginia and the Carolinas to Kentucky and Texas. Some churches have had women serving as deacons for fifty years. However, most of our churches ordain only men.

## The Viewpoint for Ordaining Only Men

Various reasons are given by those who feel the churches should only ordain men as ministers and deacons.

1. Jesus was a man and he chose twelve men to be his disciples. Therefore, only men should be ordained by the church as its spiritual leaders. Note, however, that the twelve included no Gentiles, yet the modern church is predominantly made up of Gentiles.

2. Some feel that the New Testament teaches the subordination of women—that their place of service is not to be one of leadership, in home or church.

3. Most churches prefer men, not women, as their pastors and deacons.

4. The first deacons chosen by the Jerusalem church were seven men (Acts 3) and not women.

5. In giving the qualifications for deacons in 1 Timothy 3:12, Paul wrote, "Let the deacons be the husbands of one wife." Obviously, women cannot qualify. Does this mean that a single man or a widower cannot serve as a deacon? Could Paul, himself, have met this requirement?

6. In 1 Corinthians 14:35b women are prohibited from speaking in church. This would obviously mean they should not serve as deacons or ministers.

## The Viewpoint for Ordaining Women as Well as Men

Some feel that our practice of ordaining only men is based more on tradition than on our theological or biblical interpretation.

1. An examination of the structure of 1 Timothy 3 is helpful. This passage gives the qualifications for church officers. The first section deals with what is required of bishops or pastors. Next, the passage cites the qualifications for deacons. Verse 11 begins, "The women likewise ..." (RSV). Scholars agreed that it is not certain to whom the writer is referring. It may be interpreted that "the women" are a third category of church officers. Some say they are the wives of deacons. but the passage does not refer to the wives of pastors. Others take "the women" to be a group of women who ministered in the church, perhaps women deacons. The passage is ambiguous. It could refer to deacon's wives or female deacons. The use of the word *likewise* does imply that the writer has in mind a third group of church officers. By the third century AD the churches had deaconesses who served as co-ministers with deacons. Could Phoebe

have been one of these in the New Testament period? (Rom. 16:1).

2. Examining other New Testament Scriptures we see that Paul dealt with proverbial truth and on occasion made exceptions. Sometimes on the mission field, he adapted what he felt to be the ideal to meet obvious needs in a local situation. Let's look at three such examples:

(1) Paul insisted that within the Christian church neither circumcision nor uncircumcision make any difference. (See 1 Cor. 7:19; Gal. 5:6; 6:15; Col. 3:11.) Yet, Paul had Timothy circumcised "because of the Jews" who would have been offended otherwise (Acts 16:3).

(2) Paul insisted that within the church "there is neither slave nor free man" (Col. 3:11). In the due course of history the New Testament principles of the worth of man and freedom spelled the end of human slavery. Yet, Paul counseled slaves to obey their masters as they obeyed Christ (Eph. 6:5-6; Col. 3:22; Titus 2:9). On one occasion he returned a runaway slave to his master (Onesimus to Philemon).

Paul held a lofty ideal concerning Christian liberty. Still, he took the cultural situation into account in order to not give offence and to further the gospel.

(3) We see a similar tension between proverbial truth and its exception with reference to the status of women in the early church.

In Galatians 3:28 Paul held high the principle of complete equality within the faith and in the church: In Christ "there is neither Jew nor Greek, ... there is neither male nor female." He did not mean that no such distinctions existed. Rather, he was teaching that God is no respecter of persons. Ideally, within the body of Christ (the church) all barriers are taken down: economic barriers, racial barriers, and sexual barriers. This is still a high and worthy ideal.

Yet, in the practical situation on the mission field, Paul found matters out of hand in such places as the church in Corinth. Therefore, he laid down some rules to restore order: let the women keep silent in worship (1 Cor. 14:34-35), and let the women wear veils (1 Cor. 11:5).

Were these restrictions for that local church situation or for all the churches through the centuries? Surely, the ideal of our oneness in Christ is valid. Does the spiritual ideal of Galatians 3:28 also apply to the selection of spiritual leaders such as deacons and ministers? Should qualified women as well as men be "set apart for service"?

The modern churches, like those of Paul's time, live in a tension between the biblical principles and our cultural settings—between proverbial truth and practical exceptions. Should the social customs of our time come under the judgment of the biblical ideal? Under the lordship of Christ, each congregation will want to examine its faith and practice. The goal is always to determine the mind of Christ for the church at a given point in its history.

The texts most often cited by those who feel that men as well as women may be ordained as deacons and ministers are Galatians 3:28 and Acts 2:17-18. All texts must be interpreted within the context of the total New Testament witness and applied in the life of the modern church.

Since ordination of deacons and ministers is an accepted practice among Baptists, the question of the consideration of women will continue to be with us. With our polity, it is not a decision for the denomination or any of its units to make. Churches ordain their deacons and ministers. Ultimately, it is a matter to be decided by the local church—in the light of their understanding of Scripture and under the lordship of Christ. Knowing Baptists, unanimity is not expected. Unity within diversity continues to characterize our fellowship.

## ORDINATION TO THE GOSPEL MINISTRY
### of Carol Ellen Ripley
### The Olin T. Binkley Memorial Baptist Church
### Chapel Hill, North Carolina

### THE ORDER OF CELEBRATION

Reformation Sunday                                        October 29, 1978

**PRELUDE**              Ein Feste Burg Ist Unser Gott              Pachelbel

Jesu, Meines Herzens Freud              J. S. Bach

Frances Seymour, Jan Anderson; Flutes

**CHORAL INTROIT**

"O God, in Whom We Live and Move"              Briggs

**OPENING SENTENCES**

Leader:  By all saints and witnesses we are surrounded, as by a great cloud on every side.

*People*: **Let us, following them, throw off everything that hinders us, especially the sin that clings so easily, and keep running steadily in the race we have started.**

Leader:  Let us not lose sight of Jesus, who leads us in our faith and brings it to perfection.

*People*: **For the sake of the joy which was still in the future, he endured the cross, disregarding the shamefulness of it,**

Leader:  And from now on has taken his place at the right of God's throne.

*ALL*:  Praise be to God!

**\*PROCESSIONAL HYMN**

"A Mighty Fortress Is Our God"              Luther

**\*PRAYER OF INVOCATION** *(Unison)*

O God, you will keep in perfect peace those whose minds are fixed on you; for in.returning and rest we shall be saved; in quietness and trust shall be our strength. Give us open hearts and minds as we await the discovery of your presence. Amen.

**PRESENTATION OF CAROL ELLEN RIPLEY**
**FOR ORDINATION**              James Wilde

**QUESTIONS TO THE ORDINAND AND**
   **CONGREGATION**                        Robert Seymour
**PRAYERS OF THE PEOPLE**
**ANTHEM**         "O Come Let Us Sing to the Lord"       Harris
            Children's Choir David Bibb, Accompanist
**LESSONS**             Acts 20:17-38       Lee Ann Inman
               1 Corinthians 16:8-9
**\*THE GLORIA PATRI**
**SERMON**                             Sandra R. Brown
      "Opportunities and Obstacles of the Ministry"

**\*AN AFFIRMATION OF FAITH** *(Unison)*

We find our faith in Jesus, who lives and dies and is resurrected among us, who calls us together to understand life and love as radical commitment to others.

We have faith in one God, whom Jesus trusted and called Father, who created and claimed all creatures, who enters our lives providing us with hope and redemption, shattering our complacency, demanding new life for the poor, the oppressed, and those who suffer.

We know that Jesus is seeking and saving the lost by being one of them. His body is broken; yet he is risen. He lives to bring wholeness and fullness to broken and empty lives. Because we know Jesus we can choose to be one of the poor, the oppressed and the suffering, those called to enter God's ever new creation.

We know that God's presence comes to us in community, wherever we seek to know God by doing justice. As Jesus' sisters and brothers we may call upon God to remake us, to show us our neighbor, to liberate us from evil, doubt, and greed which keep us oppressing and alone.

Because all things are possible through God's love, we proclaim the good news in this world where God is still creating and claiming those who do yet not know who God is.

**EXAMINATION**                          Robert Seymour
**CHARGE TO ORDINAND**             Catherine Snyder
**CHARGE TO THE CONGREGATION**      Robert Seymour
**\*HYMN**         "Come Down, O Love Divine"
*During the singing, all those ordained who wish to participate in the laying on of hands should come forward.*

**ORDINATION PRAYER**                                    Kadi Billman
**PRESENTATION OF STOLE**              Carolyn and Charles Ripley
**PRESENTATION OF BIBLE**                            Paul Lindsay
**INSTALLATION**                      Sue Schroeder, Biruta Nielsen
**RESPONSE OF THE CONGREGATION** *(Unison)*

> We welcome you, Carol, to this ministry, and we are grateful to God for your life. We will listen to you, learn from you, and love you. We will work with you and encourage you in keeping the faith. We gladly anticipate our shared calling to serve Christ and this community through this church. We pray that God will richly bless you as we, in turn, are blessed by you.

**THE PEACE**

> Leader:  The peace of the Lord be always with you.
> *People:*  And also with you.
> *(Here the people greet one another.)*

**CHORAL INTERLUDE**        "The Sacrifices of God"        Adult Choir
**PRESENTATION OF GIFTS**                  "So Fragile"

> A vessel, so fragile and ready to break, if I should stumble it would fall and break into a thousand pieces; lost, but for the hand of God. Guide my steps, O Lord. Help me carry it well, that I may present it at your feet, a vessel fit for your use. Amen.

**PRAYER OF THANKSGIVING**

> Leader:  Lift up your hearts.
> ***People:  We lift them up to the Lord.***
> Leader:  Let us give thanks to the Lord our God.
> ***People:  It is right to give God thanks and praise.***
> Leader:  We live to praise you, Creator, Redeemer, Sustainer, our God forever.
> ***People:  O God, who called us from death to life, we give ourselves to you; and with the community of faith through all ages, we thank you for your saving love in Jesus Christ. Amen.***

**\*INVITATION TO THE CHRISTIAN COMMUNITY**

*Persons who desire to become members of this congregation of Christ's church are invited to come forward as the hymn is sung. We welcome you to this family of faith.*

"All Who Would Valiant Be"

**CONCERNS OF THE CHRISTIAN COMMUNITY**
**THE BLESSING**      Moment of Silent Prayer      Choral Response
**POSTLUDE**      "Herr Gott, Dich Loben Alle Wir"      Pachelbel
*CONGREGATION STANDING*